JOAN BISHOP, who is Dunedin born and bred, was Southern Territory Manager for Sunbeam Appliances for more than twenty years. An award-winning food writer, Joan writes a popular monthly food column for the *Otago Daily Times* and is the author of two other highly successful cookbooks. Joan is married to a retired geologist, and they have four children and nine grandchildren between them.

JOAN BISHOP'S

NEW ZEALAND CROCKPOT & SLOW COOKER COOKBOOK

Longacre

13
33
49
75
107
123
167
181

Contents

Introduction

Slow cookers are becoming hotter and their cooking times shorter. The convenience of gentle all-day cooking is no longer guaranteed when you buy a slow cooker. Some, but not all, of the more recently manufactured slow cookers are boiling quite vigorously on LOW. With one of these models you cannot turn the slow cooker on as you leave for work in the morning and return eight or nine hours later to find delicious food waiting. It will probably be extremely overcooked. I call these slow cookers 'Speedy'.

Tougher, less expensive but more flavourful cuts of meat require gentle, lengthy cooking to produce delectably tender meat and velvety gravy. These cuts, suited to casseroling and braising, will not become meltingly tender when boiled. If you want a slow cooker that cooks slowly and gently all day, cooking meat to a succulent tenderness, there is no magical answer as to how you find one that will do this.

Choosing a slow cooker with a low wattage is no guarantee that it will cook long and slow. Wattage is detailed on the base of the appliance and is a measure of the power used by the slow cooker. I have been cooking with several of the new 'Speedy' slow cookers and the one with the lowest wattage was the one which cooked most quickly — it was the hottest.

We have run a series of simple tests using a power meter on a number of slow cookers, all with different wattages, and have concluded that choosing a slow cooker with a low wattage will not guarantee you one which cooks slowly and gently all day. There are many variables which can affect the cooking time. The size of the pot, the volume of the ingredients and the density and temperature of the food being added to the pot will all have a bearing on how quickly the food cooks. 'Speedy' slow cookers have been designed to cook at significantly higher temperatures on LOW than earlier models. They are not traditional slow cookers any more.

Shopping for a 'slow' slow cooker is a real minefield. There is no way you can tell until you get it home and try it to determine whether you have purchased a slow model or a 'Speedy' one.

On HIGH the food in the slow cooker will eventually bubble gently around the edges but on LOW it should not boil vigorously.

If your slow cooker is boiling on LOW, you will probably need to use the 'Speedy' slow cooker times given in my recipes.

I have been a slow cooker devotee for more than thirty years and I wrote my first crockpot cookbook in 1985. The biggest advantage of the slow cooker is its convenience. No pre-browning; just assemble, chop, stir, turn on the slow cooker and walk away for the day.

I hope that the days of the gentle slow cooker will return so that 'all day cooking while the cook is away' can be guaranteed.

Joan Bishop, Dunedin, July 2011

My loving thanks to family and friends whose hearty appetites and lively company have graced our table during the testing of these recipes.

Heartfelt thanks to my dear friend and fellow food writer, Mary Browne, for her ideas, enthusiasm, constructive comment and help with testing cooking times for the 'Speedy' slow cookers. And my most special thanks to my husband Tony Reay for word-processing and proof-reading without complaint. His belief in me and his gentle encouragement have been invaluable.

Important information

Which cooking time should I use?

If you are not sure which category your slow cooker falls into, you will need to gauge this for yourself from the first recipes you try. Keep a close watch on the food in the slow cooker during the late stage of cooking to see if it needs more or less cooking than the suggested time. This should give you a fairly good idea as to which set of times are most suited to your slow cooker.

Use cooking times provided as a guideline. Slow cookers all vary. The time that food takes to cook depends on the type of food, the temperature of the food when placed in the slow cooker, the cut size of the food and how full the cooker is. All will affect the cooking time.

Cooking times for crockpots & slow cookers

In some recipes, particularly those cooked on LOW, the slowness of the cooking means that timing is not so important. Food does not overheat or boil and will not burn. Some recipes have a wide variation in cooking time, for example 'Cook on low for 7–8 hours'. This indicates that the food will be cooked in seven hours but an extra hour will not overcook it. Breads, cakes and puddings need careful timing and should be removed from the slow cooker as soon as they are cooked.

Cooking times for 'Speedy' slow cookers

The new 'Speedy' slow cookers are cooking at significantly higher temperatures than earlier models and food will boil, and can easily overcook and burn.

Timing is quite critical. In many recipes food cannot be left for an extra hour or two even on LOW. Once the food is cooked if you are not ready to serve immediately, switch to 'Keep Warm' if this setting is available or turn the slow cooker to OFF and it will retain its heat for about 30 minutes. With cakes and puddings, remove them from the slow cooker as soon as you know they are done.

Lifting the lid

To avoid heat loss, refrain from lifting the lid during the cooking process. The heat level in a slow cooker builds up slowly and every time the lid is lifted the temperature falls — consequently the food takes longer to cook. After checking for doneness, get the lid on as quickly as possible.

Stirring

Stirring during cooking is unnecessary if on LOW and only occasionally needed on HIGH. Vegetable or bean stews are the only recipes that may benefit from a stir after three or four hours cooking on HIGH.

Slow cookers and crockpots have side coil heating elements and cook at relatively low temperatures so food does not stick or burn on the bottom or bubble over. If you would like to stir, do, but get the lid back on fast to prevent heat loss.

Preheating

Placing food in a warm cooker means that the temperature at which food starts to cook will be reached more quickly. It is absolutely essential that the slow cooker is pre-heated before baking or when adding hot liquid to the cooker, otherwise the ceramic liner could crack.

Pre-browning meat & chicken

This is not necessary for flavour. The only other reason to pre-brown in a frying pan is to eliminate excess fat. However, excess fat can also be eliminated quickly and easily by trimming fat from the meat before cooking, discarding chicken skin and choosing sausages which are not overly fatty. (See page 101.)

High or low?

Cooking for one hour on HIGH is equivalent to cooking for two hours on LOW. If you need to speed up the cooking time for a recipe being cooked on LOW, turn the slow cooker to HIGH to halve the remaining cooking time.

Liquid

During cooking, steam condenses on the lid then trickles down to the rim of the ceramic bowl and forms a vapour seal around the lid preventing steam from escaping. Because of this, heat, flavour and cooking smells are retained and evaporation does not take place. Usually a cup or more of liquid forms in the slow cooker during cooking.

However, with the new 'Speedy' slow cookers this does not always happen. If the vapour seal does not occur, evaporation will take place and more liquid may need to be added. If so, add hot liquid to the slow cooker, cold could crack the ceramic liner.

How full?

Because slow cookers have side coil heating elements to heat the food efficiently they should be at least half to three-quarters full. There should however, be a gap of 2–4 cm between the top of the food and the rim of the cooker.

Thickening

The dishes can be thickened either at the beginning or at the end of the cooking process. Use flour at the beginning or stir in a cornflour paste at the end. The liquid used to make the paste need not be water. Chicken, beef or vegetable stock, wines, spirits or juices all add extra flavour. Once the cornflour paste is stirred in, turn the control to HIGH and cook for another 20–30 minutes. Alternatively drain the liquid into a saucepan, add the cornflour paste and bring to the boil on the stove or in a microwave, stirring until smooth and thickened.

Onions

Onions take a long time to cook in the slow cooker, especially on LOW.

For soups and other dishes cooked on HIGH this is not such a problem although the onions still need to be finely chopped. For dishes with shorter cooking times or for those recipes that cook on LOW, I use only a small amount of onion, substitute onion salt for onion, or stir in chopped chives or spring onions once cooking is complete. If you have time and don't mind the extra dishes you can sauté the onion in a pan prior to putting it in the slow cooker.

Root vegetables

Root vegetables, potatoes, carrots, parsnips etc are dense, and often take longer to cook than meat. When adding to one pot casseroles cut them into small same size pieces, 1–2 cm, and place at the bottom or sides of the slow cooker.

Pulses

The slow cooker is the best way that I know of to cook pulses. No presoaking is needed. (See Vegetarian and Pulses, page 49.)

Seasoning

Flavours can become diluted with long slow cooking as none of the liquid inside the cooker evaporates. Therefore more seasoning is needed than for other methods of cooking. Dried herbs are best added at the beginning of the cooking process whereas fresh herbs give more pizzazz when added during the final 30 minutes.

Add both in greater quantities than you would normally use. Before serving, taste and if necessary add more seasoning.

Trivet

A trivet is required in a number of recipes to

raise the dish off the bottom of the cooker, allowing a better circulation of air or water. If a trivet is not available use the screw-top ring of a preserving jar, an upturned saucer, a metal biscuit cutter or three $2 coins placed strategically under the container.

Foil straps

A band of folded aluminium foil about 5cm wide makes it much easier to lift out hot cake tins and pudding basins. Fold a long piece of aluminium foil (about 70cm) in half lengthways, then in half again lengthways. Placed under the container, this band enables you to lift hot containers out of the cooker with reasonable ease.

Adapting your own recipes

Slow cooker cooking is easy and uncomplicated but nevertheless different from conventional cooking. Initially tailor made recipes are a good idea but once a few basic do's and don'ts are understood and you become familiar with what the slow cooker can do you can easily adapt your own recipes.

Portable

A slow cooker is compact and easily transportable. It can go on holiday with you. Take it in the caravan or to the bach.

Slow cookers do emit some heat so when temperatures are soaring pick up the slow cooker and put it in the laundry. Turn it on and shut the door.

Preparation

Organise the evening meal at a time to suit you, early in the day or the night before.

If preparing food the night before, refrigerate it in the ceramic pot overnight. Place it in the cold slow cooker, and add 30 minutes to your projected cooking time.

Frozen foods

Frozen foods should be thoroughly thawed before being placed in the cooker. As frozen vegetables have been blanched, the cooking times are shorter than those of fresh vegetables. Usually, thawed frozen vegetables are added towards the end of the cooking process.

Economy

Cooking in the slow cooker is economical and environmentally friendly.

One of the reasons that the slow cooker is so energy efficient is that the wattage is low (the wattage is given on the base of the appliance) and is equivalent to two or three light bulbs.

Red lentil & carrot soup (see p. 30)

Soups

The slow cooker is an ideal vessel for cooking soups. Almost all soups, because they contain vegetables or dried beans and lentils, need to be cooked on high. Dried beans do not need soaking prior to cooking — they can be added to the slow cooker with the other ingredients. (For more detailed information on cooking dried beans, see p. 50.)

Once a bean soup is cooked, if it's not as thick as you would like it to be, mash up or purée some of the liquid and beans in a food processor or blender, then stir back into the soup.

Don't overfill the slow cooker: there should be a gap of 3–4 cm between the level of the food and the rim of the slow cooker.

Soups with a long cooking time can be cooked overnight.

Chicken stock

The best stock is one you make yourself, and it is simple to make good chicken stock. Supermarkets usually have chicken carcasses or frames for very reasonable prices.

2 or 3 raw chicken carcasses with the livers removed (as they can impart a bitter flavour)
1 onion, finely chopped
1 carrot, peeled and finely chopped
2 celery stalks, finely sliced
2 tsp salt
large sprig thyme
2 bay leaves
boiling water to cover

1. Preheat the slow cooker for 20 minutes.
2. Place all the ingredients in the slow cooker, cover with lid and cook according to the times and settings specified.
3. Cool, and strain the stock through a sieve.

CROCKPOT	**high for 6–7 hours**
SLOW COOKER	**high for 6–7 hours**
SPEEDY SLOW COOKER	**high for 5–6 hours**

Beef Stock

Homemade beef stock is simple and inexpensive to make. A good stock is the basis of many dishes and instant stock cubes or powders do not give anywhere near the same depth of flavour.

1. Preheat the slow cooker for 20 minutes.
2. Chop beef bones into small pieces, to extract maximum flavour. (Your butcher can do this for you.)
3. Place all ingredients in the slow cooker with sufficient boiling water to barely cover.
4. Cover with lid and cook according to the times and settings specified.
5. Strain and cool. Skim off any fat.

CROCKPOT	high for 6–7 hours
SLOW COOKER	high for 6–7 hours
SPEEDY SLOW COOKER	high for 5–6 hours

- 1½ kg meaty beef bones
- 2 large carrots, peeled and finely chopped
- 2 large onions, finely chopped
- 2 stalks celery, finely sliced
- 2 bay leaves
- 1 large sprig thyme
- 2 large stalks parsley
- 2 tsp salt
- 6 black peppercorns
- 6 whole cloves
- boiling water

Bacon and lentil soup

The lentils add an earthy flavour and appealing texture to this warming, homely soup.

1. Preheat the slow cooker for 20 minutes.
2. Place bacon, onion, garlic, carrots, tomatoes, tomato paste and red wine in the slow cooker.
3. Wash lentils thoroughly, drain and add to the slow cooker. Pour in the boiling stock and stir.
4. Cover with lid and cook according to the times and settings specified.
5. Check seasoning, adding salt if necessary.
6. Ladle soup into bowls and garnish with Parmesan shavings.

CROCKPOT	**high for 6–7 hours**
SLOW COOKER	**high for 6–7 hours**
SPEEDY SLOW COOKER	**high for 4½–5½ hours**

4 lean bacon rashers, trimmed and chopped
1 medium onion, finely chopped
3 cloves garlic, crushed
2 medium carrots, peeled and diced into 1 cm cubes
1 x 400 g can diced tomatoes in juice
2 Tbsp tomato paste
½ cup red wine
1 cup split red lentils
5 cups boiling vegetable or chicken stock
salt
shaved Parmesan cheese

SERVES 4–6

Bean and mushroom soup

Richly flavoured with mushrooms, this soup is so good, yet so simple to prepare. It is one of my favourites.

1. Preheat the slow cooker for 20 minutes.
2. Place dried mushrooms in a bowl and pour boiling water over them. Let them stand for 20–30 minutes.
3. Place lima beans in the slow cooker. Add onion, tomatoes, soy sauce, beef stock and dried mushrooms and their soaking liquid, discarding stems.
4. Cover with lid and cook according to the times and settings specified.
5. Forty-five minutes prior to the completion of the cooking process, add Portabello mushrooms. Replace the lid and cook for the final three-quarters of an hour.
6. Serve hot with a tablespoon of yoghurt swirled into each soup bowl.

20 g dried shiitake mushrooms
¾ cup boiling water
1½ cups dried baby lima beans, washed and drained
1 medium onion, finely chopped
1 x 400 g can diced tomatoes in juice
2 Tbsp soy sauce
6 cups beef stock, hot
220 g Portabello mushrooms, wiped and sliced thinly
½ cup thick, plain yoghurt to serve

SERVES 5–6

CROCKPOT	**high for 6–7 hours**
SLOW COOKER	**high for 6–7 hours**
SPEEDY SLOW COOKER	**high for 5–6 hours**

Beef, bacon and shiitake mushroom soup

The deliciously aromatic liquid of this soup is chock-full of flavourful surprises: tender strips of beef, diced bacon, cubed potato, sliced cultivated mushrooms and shiitake mushrooms. If served with a good crusty bread, this is a complete meal in itself.

Dried shiitake mushrooms are available in Asian food stores and many large supermarkets. They need to be soaked in warm water for at least half an hour before using.

1. Preheat the slow cooker for 20 minutes.
2. Remove any excess fat from the steak and set aside.
3. Soak shiitake mushrooms in the warm water for at least 30 minutes.
4. Place onion, garlic, bacon, potatoes, tomatoes and beef stock in the slow cooker.
5. Slice shiitake mushrooms, discarding stems. Add sliced shiitake mushrooms and the soaking water to the slow cooker.
6. Cover with lid and cook according to the times and settings specified.
7. Grill, barbecue or pan fry the rump steak. I usually cook it medium rare as it does continue to cook a little once added to the soup.
8. Cool the steak and slice into thin strips.

250 g rump steak
30 g dried shiitake mushrooms
1 cup warm water
1 large onion, finely chopped
2 cloves garlic, crushed
3 rashers lean bacon, trimmed and diced
3 medium potatoes (600 g), peeled and diced into 1 cm cubes
1 x 400 g can diced tomatoes in juice
5 cups beef stock, hot

9 Thirty minutes prior to the end of cooking time, add steak and Portabello mushrooms to the slow cooker and continue to cook for the final half hour. Serve hot.

200 g Portabello mushrooms, sliced thinly

SERVES 8

CROCKPOT	high for 5–6 hours
SLOW COOKER	high for 5–6 hours
SPEEDY SLOW COOKER	high for 4½–5 hours

Bean and vegetable soup

A hearty, chunky soup which makes a perfect one-dish meal for a cold winter's night. I have made this soup with black beans and black-eyed beans in place of the haricot beans. The black beans turn the soup a steely, grey-black colour which is not unattractive, just different.

1. Preheat the slow cooker for 20 minutes.
2. Place well-drained beans in the slow cooker.
3. Dice parsnip and carrots into small cubes (1 cm) and place in the slow cooker.
4. Add onion, garlic, tomato paste, tomatoes, cayenne pepper, brown sugar, basil and beef stock. Stir well.
5. Cover with lid and cook according to the times and settings specified.
6. Check seasoning, adding salt if necessary.
7. Ladle the soup into bowls and sprinkle with grated Parmesan cheese.

CROCKPOT	high for 8–9 hours
SLOW COOKER	high for 7½–8 hours
SPEEDY SLOW COOKER	high for 6–7 hours

220 g dried haricot beans, washed
1 large parsnip (300 g), peeled
2 medium carrots (250 g), peeled
1 large onion, finely chopped
2 cloves garlic, crushed
½ cup tomato paste
1 x 400 g can diced tomatoes in juice
¼–½ tsp cayenne pepper
1 tsp brown sugar
2 tsp dried basil
6 cups beef or vegetable stock, hot
salt
grated Parmesan cheese to serve

SERVES 8–9

Curried pumpkin soup

Pumpkin soup, with its rich flavour, creamy texture and glorious colour, is a universal favourite. The light evaporated milk has all the rich creaminess of cream but only a fraction of the calories.

1. Preheat the slow cooker for 20 minutes.
2. Place pumpkin and potato in the slow cooker.
3. Add tomatoes, onion, pepper and chicken stock.
4. Cover with lid and cook according to the times and settings specified.
5. Add curry powder and brown sugar.
6. Purée using a stick blender, or process in a food processor or blender.
7. Return to the slow cooker and add evaporated milk. Stir well and check seasoning, adding salt if necessary.
8. Reheat but do not boil. Serve sprinkled with chopped chives.

CROCKPOT	**high for 5–7 hours**
SLOW COOKER	**high for 5–7 hours**
SPEEDY SLOW COOKER	**high for 4½–5 hours**

1 kg pumpkin, peeled and diced into 2 cm cubes
1 large potato, peeled and diced into 2 cm cubes
1 x 400 g can diced tomatoes in juice
1 onion, finely chopped
freshly ground black pepper
6 cups chicken stock, hot
1½ tsp curry powder
2 tsp brown sugar
½ cup light and creamy evaporated milk
salt
chopped chives to garnish

SERVES 8–10

Golden pea soup with bacon

Split peas give this soup a lusciously thick consistency, making a substantial and comforting meal for a chilly winter's day.

If preferred, use bacon bones (about 600 g), or bacon rashers (250 g), trimmed and chopped in place of the bacon hock. Green split peas can replace the yellow but of course the colour will not be golden.

1. Preheat the slow cooker for 20 minutes.
2. Place split peas, hock, carrot, onion, thyme and stock in the slow cooker.
3. Cover with lid and cook according to the times and settings specified.
4. Fifteen minutes before the end of the cooking process, remove hock from the slow cooker. Peel off rind and discard. Shred meat from the bone, remove any fat and return meat to the slow cooker. Thin the soup with a little more stock if it is too thick.
5. Stir in spinach and sherry. Cover with lid and cook for 15 minutes more. Season with salt and pepper.
6. Serve hot with cheese croutons.
7. To make croutons, place 10 baguette slices on a baking tray. Spray lightly with olive oil and sprinkle with grated tasty cheese. Bake at 200°C until cheese melts.

400 g yellow split peas
1 bacon hock
1 large carrot, peeled and diced into 1 cm cubes
1 medium onion, finely chopped
2 sprigs fresh thyme, or 1 tsp dried
7–8 cups hot chicken or vegetable stock
1 cup finely chopped spinach leaves
2 Tbsp sherry (optional)
salt and pepper

SERVES 8–10

CROCKPOT	**high for 6–7 hours**
SLOW COOKER	**high for 6–7 hours**
SPEEDY SLOW COOKER	**high for 4¾–5½ hours**

Kumara and carrot soup

Coconut milk gives a smooth richness to this velvety golden soup and the red curry paste adds a mild spiciness.

1. Pre-heat cooker for 20 minutes.
2. Place carrots, onion, garlic, red curry paste, ginger, brown sugar, cinnamon, chicken stock and coconut milk in the slow cooker.
3. Cover with lid and cook following the times and settings specified.
4. Cool slightly and puree using a stick blender or process in a food processor or blender.
5. Check seasoning, adding salt if necessary.
6. Serve garnished with chopped chives.

CROCKPOT	**high for 6–7 hours**
SLOW COOKER	**high for 6–7 hours**
SPEEDY SLOW COOKER	**high for 5–5½ hours**

700 g kumara, peeled and diced into 2–3cm cubes
500 g carrots, peeled and finely diced
1 medium onion, finely chopped
3 cloves garlic, crushed
2 Tbsp Thai red curry paste
1 tsp each ground ginger and brown sugar
½ tsp ground cinnamon
6 cups chicken stock, hot
1 x 400 ml can coconut milk
salt
chopped chives to garnish

SERVES 6–7

Kumara and pumpkin soup with peanuts

These vegetables complement each other well, and the addition of peanut butter gives the soup a rich flavour and a smooth texture. A real winner.

1. Preheat the slow cooker for 20 minutes.
2. Place pumpkin, kumara, onion and chicken stock in the slow cooker. Cover with lid and cook according to the times and settings specified.
3. Cool slightly and purée using a stick blender, or process in a food processor or blender, and return to the slow cooker.
4. Stir in the peanut butter.
5. Cover with lid and continue to cook on high for 30–40 minutes until hot.
6. Check seasoning, adding salt if necessary.
7. This is a fairly thick soup. If desired, thin with a little milk, cream or chicken stock.
8. Serve hot, garnished with a sprinkling of chopped peanuts.

CROCKPOT	**high for 5–6 hours**
SLOW COOKER	**high for 5–6 hours**
SPEEDY SLOW COOKER	**high for 4–4½ hours**

700 g pumpkin, peeled and diced into 2–3 cm cubes
700 g kumara, peeled and diced into 2–3 cm cubes
1 onion, finely chopped
6 cups chicken stock, hot
¾ cup smooth peanut butter
salt
chopped roasted, unsalted peanuts to garnish

SERVES 7–8

Lamb and lentil broth

Lamb shanks, vegetables and lentils simmer together to make a hearty, inexpensive soup. Once the cooking is complete, the tender, flavourful meat is removed from the bone and returned to the broth.

Lamb shanks are usually sold with the leg bone cut in half. When preparing them for the slow cooker, continue the cut and slice into two pieces.

1. Preheat slow cooker for 20 minutes.
2. Trim any fat from shanks and place shanks in slow cooker.
3. Add onion, garlic, carrots, parsnip, lentils, chilli, cumin, ginger and vegetable stock.
4. Cover with lid and cook according to the times and settings specified.
5. Remove shanks, cut meat from the bone into small pieces and return to the slow cooker.
6. Check seasoning, adding salt if necessary.
7. Serve hot, sprinkled with chopped parsley.

CROCKPOT	**high for 6–8 hours**
SLOW COOKER	**high for 6–8 hours**
SPEEDY SLOW COOKER	**high for 5–6 hours**

2 lamb shanks, halved
1 large onion, finely chopped
3 cloves garlic, crushed
2 medium carrots, peeled and diced into 1 cm cubes
1 medium parsnip, peeled and diced into 1 cm cubes
300 g lentils, washed and drained
½ tsp prepared, chopped chilli
1½ tsp ground cumin
1½ tsp ground ginger
6 cups vegetable stock, hot
salt
chopped parsley to garnish

SERVES 6

Leek and potato soup

This recipe is based on the classic French soup, vichyssoise.

3 large leeks (750 g)
400 g potatoes, peeled and diced into 1 cm cubes
black pepper
½ tsp ground nutmeg
7 cups chicken stock, hot
1¼ cups light and creamy evaporated milk
chives, finely chopped

SERVES 8–10

1. Preheat slow cooker for 20 minutes.
2. Trim leeks to remove tough tops and outer leaves. Wash thoroughly and slice thinly, including some of the green part. Place sliced leeks in the slow cooker.
3. Add the potatoes, pepper, nutmeg and chicken stock.
4. Cover with lid and cook according to the times and settings specified.
5. Purée the soup using a stick blender, or process in a food processor or blender. Return to the slow cooker.
6. Add evaporated milk. Replace the lid and continue to cook on high until the soup is heated through. Do not boil.
7. Serve sprinkled with chives.

CROCKPOT	**high for 5–7 hours**
SLOW COOKER	**high for 5–7 hours**
SPEEDY SLOW COOKER	**high for 4½–5 hours**

Old-fashioned vegetable soup

A cold-weather soup to warm the heart and soul.

1. Preheat slow cooker for 20 minutes.
2. Trim fat off meat. Place meat and bones in the slow cooker.
3. Combine remaining ingredients (except salt and parsley) in the slow cooker.
4. Cover with lid and cook according to the times and settings specified.
5. Lift bones from the slow cooker. Remove the lean meat from the bones. Cut meat into small pieces and return to the slow cooker. Discard bones.
6. Remove any fat from the surface of the soup with a spoon or paper towel. Check seasoning, and add salt if necessary.
7. Serve sprinkled with chopped parsley.

CROCKPOT	**high for 6–8 hours**
SLOW COOKER	**high for 6–8 hours**
SPEEDY SLOW COOKER	**high for 5–6 hours**

500 g lamb or mutton neck chops or beef shin on the bone
2 medium carrots, peeled and finely chopped
1 large onion, finely chopped
2 stalks celery, finely sliced
2 cups chopped vegetables, e.g. potato, pumpkin, parsnip, leek, kumara
⅓ cup lentils
½ cup soup mix
7 cups beef stock, hot
2 Tbsp Worcester sauce
3 Tbsp tomato paste
1 tsp dried thyme
salt
chopped parsley to garnish

SERVES 6–8

Potato and corn chowder

Delicious and substantial, this homely soup is a meal-in-a-bowl, especially if served with hot crusty bread.

1 onion, finely chopped
3 large potatoes (600 g), peeled and diced into 1 cm cubes
2 cloves garlic, crushed
3 Tbsp raw rice, preferably short grain
1 tsp prepared, chopped chilli
1½ tsp smoked paprika
500 g whole kernel corn, thawed if frozen
1 red capsicum, de-seeded and finely sliced
6 cups chicken or vegetable stock, hot
1¼ cups light and creamy evaporated milk
salt
2 Tbsp chopped fresh parsley to garnish

SERVES 8

1. Preheat the slow cooker for 20 minutes.
2. Combine onion, potatoes, garlic, rice, chilli, smoked paprika, corn, capsicum and chicken stock in the slow cooker, and stir.
3. Cover with lid and cook according to the times and settings specified.
4. Add evaporated milk and stir. Reheat until hot but do not boil.
5. Check seasoning, and add salt if necessary.
6. Serve hot, sprinkled with chopped parsley.

CROCKPOT	**high for 8–9 hours**
SLOW COOKER	**high for 7½–8½ hours**
SPEEDY SLOW COOKER	**high for 6–7 hours**

Red lentil and carrot soup with lemon and parsley yoghurt

The lentils, subtly flavoured with herbs and spices, cook to a purée giving this soup a thick and luscious consistency. Lentils do not need soaking prior to cooking but they should be washed thoroughly.

Warm naan or pitta bread are good accompaniments.

1 medium onion, finely chopped
3 cloves garlic, crushed
1 tsp each, dried basil, turmeric and ground cumin
1 Tbsp minced ginger
2 large carrots (300 g), peeled and diced into 1 cm cubes
7 cups vegetable stock, hot
300 g split red lentils
2 Tbsp tomato paste
salt

Lemon & parsley yoghurt

½ cup Greek style, yoghurt
2 Tbsp chopped fresh parsley
grated zest of one lemon

SERVES 6

1. Preheat the cooker for 20 minutes.
2. Combine onion, garlic, basil, turmeric, cumin, ginger, carrots, stock, lentils and tomato paste in the cooker and mix well.
3. Cover with lid and cook following the times and settings specified.
4. Check seasoning, adding salt if necessary.
5. Cool a little and purée in a food processor, blender or with a stick blender. Reheat.
6. In a small bowl mix the yoghurt, parsley and lemon zest together.
7. Serve the soup piping hot with a spoonful of Lemon & parsley yoghurt swirled on top.

CROCKPOT	high for 5–6 hours
SLOW COOKER	high for 5–6 hours
SPEEDY SLOW COOKER	high for 4–5 hours

Smoky pumpkin and apple soup

This velvety soup is infused with a delicate smoky flavour. Do not, however, add too much smoked paprika as the flavour of the pumpkin and apples should be apparent. Soups that are puréed should be thoroughly cooked before being processed as hard, partly cooked vegetables will result in a lumpy purée.

If Granny Smith apples are unavailable, use another eating apple, preferably one that's not too sweet.

1 kg peeled pumpkin, diced into 2 cm cubes
1 onion, finely chopped
3 Granny Smith apples (500 g), peeled, cored and diced into 2–3 cm cubes
1 Tbsp minced ginger
¾ tsp prepared, chopped chilli
5 cups chicken stock, hot
1¼ tsp sweet smoked paprika
salt
chopped parsley to garnish

1. Preheat the slow cooker for 20 minutes.
2. Place pumpkin, onion, apples, ginger and chilli in the slow cooker and add chicken stock.
3. Cover with lid and cook according to the times and settings specified.
4. Cool slightly and purée using a stick blender, or process in a food processor or blender, and return to the slow cooker.
5. Add the smoked paprika and reheat the soup.
6. Check seasoning, and add salt if necessary.
7. Serve hot, garnished with chopped parsley.

SERVES 8

CROCKPOT	**high for 5–7 hours**
SLOW COOKER	**high for 5–7 hours**
SPEEDY SLOW COOKER	**high for 4–4½ hours**

Ratatouille (see p. 38)

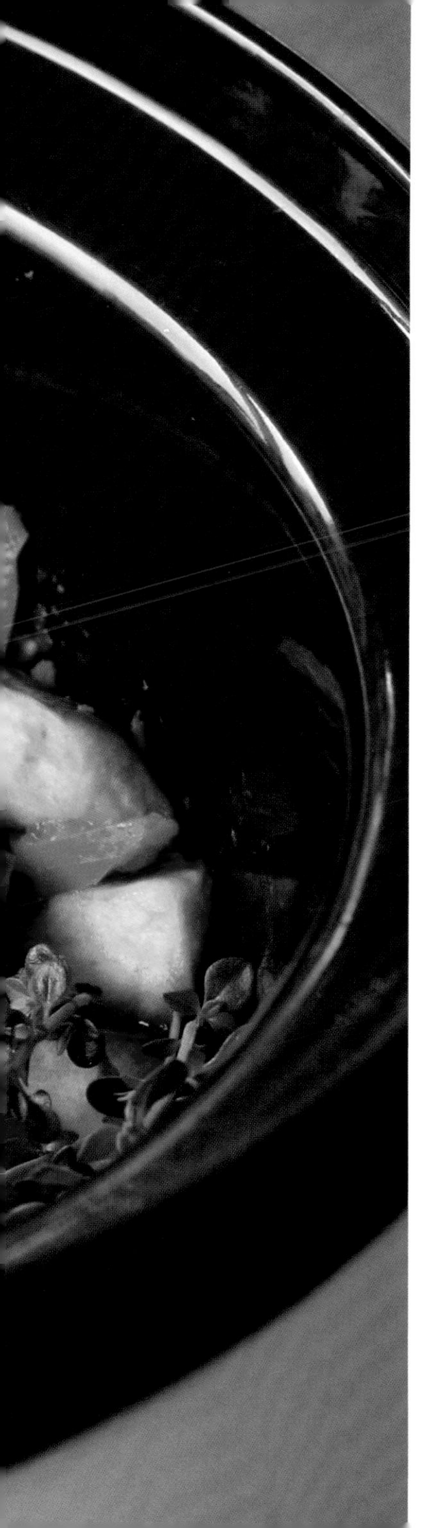

Vegetables

I like crisp, crunchy, lightly cooked green vegetables. Slow cooking cannot achieve this result and so I do not recommend using the slow cooker for cooking green vegetables.

Many root vegetables can be cooked very successfully in the slow cooker but they need to be cooked on high.

Frozen vegetables can be added to the slow cooker during the last 30 minutes of cooking time but they must be thawed before adding, otherwise they lower the temperature too much.

Carrots with marmalade and mint

Carrots are a great standby winter vegetable, especially if they are prepared imaginatively. Marmalade and mint give these carrots real pizzazz. Choose small carrots as they are more likely to be sweet and tender.

1. Preheat slow cooker for 20 minutes.
2. Scatter carrots over the base of the slow cooker.
3. Pour the hot stock over the carrots and ensure they are evenly distributed in the slow cooker.
4. Cover with lid and cook according to the times and settings specified.
5. When the carrots are tender, drain off the stock and stir in the marmalade, oil and mint.

450 g carrots, peeled and cut into thin rings
vegetable or chicken stock, hot, to cover
2 Tbsp marmalade
1 Tbsp olive oil
2 Tbsp freshly chopped mint

SERVES 4–5

CROCKPOT	**high for 1¾–2 hours**
SLOW COOKER	**high for 1¾ hours**
SPEEDY SLOW COOKER	**high for 1½ hours**

Casserole of pumpkin and kumara

This medley of colourful vegetables is especially delicious with roasts or grills. The pumpkin and kumara cook more slowly than the other vegetables so cut into a small dice. The courgettes and red capsicum can be cut into slightly larger pieces.

1. Combine pumpkin, kumara, red capsicum, courgettes, onion and garlic in the slow cooker.
2. Spoon tomato paste and tomatoes onto the vegetables.
3. Stir thoroughly so that the tomato paste and tomatoes are mixed evenly through the vegetables.
4. Cover with lid and cook according to the times and settings specified.
5. Sprinkle with chopped fresh herbs and serve.

CROCKPOT	**high for 3½–3¾ hours**
SLOW COOKER	**high for 3¼–3½ hours**
SPEEDY SLOW COOKER	**high for 2¾–3 hours**

400 g peeled pumpkin, diced into 2 cm cubes
400 g peeled kumara (1 large), diced into 2 cm cubes
1 large red capsicum, de-seeded and sliced
2 medium courgettes, sliced
1 small red onion, finely chopped
3 cloves garlic, crushed
¼ cup tomato paste
1 x 400 g can diced tomatoes in juice
3 Tbsp chopped fresh herbs

SERVES 6–7

Honey and lemon kumara

The timing for vegetable dishes is not as flexible as for many other dishes. The kumara should not be cooked to a mush but should remain in whole pieces, lightly coated with the lemony syrup.

For this recipe I like to use the golden kumara variety as it is such a gorgeous colour and does not discolour once peeled. It has longer, thinner tubers than the red variety and of course the skin and flesh are golden.

1. Peel kumara and dice into 1 cm cubes.
2. Place in the slow cooker and sprinkle with lemon zest.
3. In a small bowl combine lemon juice, honey and butter and heat in a microwave or over hot water until melted.
4. Pour this mixture over the kumara, sprinkle with salt and pepper and toss to mix.
5. Cover with lid and cook according to the times and settings specified.

600 g kumara
grated zest of ½ lemon
2 Tbsp lemon juice
2 tsp honey
1 Tbsp butter
½ tsp salt
freshly ground black pepper

SERVES 4

CROCKPOT	**high for approx 2 hours**
SLOW COOKER	**high for 1¾–2 hours**
SPEEDY SLOW COOKER	**high for 1½ hours**

Parsnip with apple and coriander

Rich and sweet, and given an intriguing freshness by the apple, this dish is ideal for serving with a casserole.

Choose young, small parsnips as they have a much sweeter, nuttier taste. If possible, use a tart dessert apple such as Granny Smith.

450 g parsnip
1 large (220 g) dessert apple
chicken stock, hot, to cover
2 tsp raw sugar
¾ tsp ground coriander
1 Tbsp olive oil
salt
chopped parsley

SERVES 4

1. Preheat slow cooker for 20 minutes.
2. Wash and peel parsnips. Slice into thin rounds and place in the slow cooker.
3. Peel, core and thickly slice the apple and add to the slow cooker.
4. Barely cover the parsnip and apple with the hot chicken stock.
5. Cover with lid and cook according to the times and settings specified.
6. Drain off the chicken stock. Sprinkle parsnips and apples with sugar and coriander and toss to mix.
7. Stir in the olive oil and check the seasoning, adding salt if necessary.
8. Sprinkle with parsley and serve.

CROCKPOT	**high for 1¾–2 hours**
SLOW COOKER	**high for 1¾ hours**
SPEEDY SLOW COOKER	**high for 1½ hours**

Ratatouille

During late summer and early autumn these vegetables are at their peak and when combined they make a wonderful vegetable casserole.

1 large or 2 small aubergines (about 600 g)
1 small red onion, finely chopped
4 cloves garlic, crushed
2 medium red capsicums, de-seeded and thinly sliced
2 Tbsp olive oil
2 Tbsp tomato paste
1 x 400 g can diced tomatoes in juice
salt and pepper
2 Tbsp chopped fresh thyme

1. Wash and trim the aubergine and dice into 2–3 cm cubes.
2. Combine aubergine, onion, garlic and red capsicums in the slow cooker.
3. In a small bowl mix together olive oil, tomato paste and the tomatoes until well blended.
4. Spoon mixture over the vegetables in the slow cooker and stir well to combine, making sure all the vegetable pieces are well coated.
5. Cover with lid and cook according to the times and settings specified.
6. Check seasoning – you will probably need to add salt and pepper.
7. Sprinkle with the chopped thyme and serve.

SERVES 4–5

CROCKPOT	**high for 3½–3¾ hours**
SLOW COOKER	**high for 3½ hours**
SPEEDY SLOW COOKER	**high for 3 hours**

Red cabbage with apple and dill

Timing is more crucial for this recipe than for most, but this will vary depending on how finely the cabbage is cut. The cabbage should retain a little crispness and the apple slices should remain whole, and not cooked to a pulp.

½ medium red cabbage (600 g)
2 medium dessert apples (300 g)
2 Tbsp honey
2 Tbsp wine vinegar
1 Tbsp butter
½ tsp onion salt
freshly ground black pepper
1½ tsp dill seeds
¼ cup finely chopped chives or spring onions

1. Finely shred cabbage and place in the cooker.
2. Peel, core and slice apples and add to the cooker.
3. In a small bowl combine honey, wine vinegar and butter. Melt in a microwave or over hot water.
4. Pour this mixture into the slow cooker and add onion salt, pepper and dill seeds. Toss to mix well.
5. Cover with lid and cook following the times and settings specified.
6. Sprinkle with chopped chives or spring onions and serve.

SERVES 6

CROCKPOT	**high for 1¾–2¼ hours**
SLOW COOKER	**high for 1¾–2 hours**
SPEEDY SLOW COOKER	**high for 1½ hours**

Potato hot pot

These potatoes, subtly spiced with chilli and paprika and cooked until tender in a tomato-based sauce, are perfect to serve with roast or barbecue meats or chicken. Waxy potatoes retain their shape when cooked. Look for Nadines, Draga or Red King Edward or use an all purpose potato like Desiree or Maris Anchor.

1 Preheat the slow cooker for 20 minutes.
2 Place onions, potatoes, capsicum and garlic in the slow cooker.
3 In a bowl, combine the tomatoes, tomato paste, chilli, paprika and stock. Mix well and pour over the vegetables. Stir to combine.
4 Cover with lid and cook according to the times and settings specified.
5 Add the olives 30 minutes before the cooking time is completed and stir gently.
6 Cover with lid and cook for the final half hour. Taste and add salt if necessary.
7 Stir in the parsley and serve.

CROCKPOT	**high for 5½–6 hours**
SLOW COOKER	**high for 4–4½ hours**
SPEEDY SLOW COOKER	**high for 3¾–4½ hours**

1 small onion, finely chopped
1 kg waxy potatoes, peeled and diced into 2 cm cubes
1 red capsicum, de-seeded and cut into 2 cm pieces
3 cloves garlic crushed
1x 400 g can diced tomatoes in juice
1 Tbsp tomato paste
½–¾ tsp prepared chilli
1 tsp sweet smoked paprika
¾ cup hot vegetable or chicken stock
1/2 cup green or black olives (optional)
salt
½ cup roughly chopped flat leaf parsley

SERVES 4–6 AS A SIDE DISH

Sweet and sour pumpkin

This is a tasty way to serve pumpkin.

1. Peel pumpkin, discard seeds, cut into 2 cm cubes and place in slow cooker.
2. Add oil, garlic, raw sugar, salt and vinegar to the slow cooker and toss pumpkin very thoroughly, so that the oil coats all surfaces.
3. Cover with lid and cook according to the times and settings specified or until pumpkin is tender but not mushy.
4. Remove lid and continue cooking for about 10 minutes so that any liquid remaining in the slow cooker evaporates.
5. Sprinkle with peanuts (optional) and serve hot.

700 g pumpkin
2 tsp olive oil
2 cloves garlic, crushed
1½ Tbsp raw sugar
½ tsp salt
2½ Tbsp white or red wine vinegar
¼ cup chopped roasted, unsalted peanuts (optional)

SERVES 4

CROCKPOT	**high for approx 3½ hours**
SLOW COOKER	**high for 3 hours**
SPEEDY SLOW COOKER	**high for 2½ hours**

Pilaf with Saffron and Currants (see p. 47)

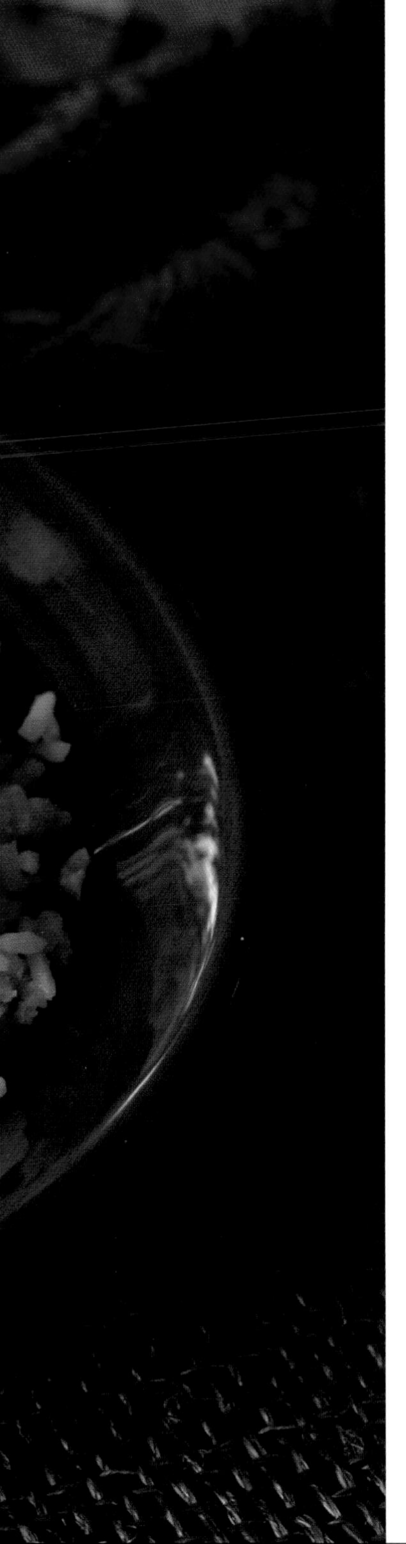

Rice

Some types of rice can be cooked very effectively in your slow cooker. Well-cooked rice absorbs its liquid; the grains swell and retain all the flavours. (The slow cooker, however, does not cook brown rice successfully.)

A cup of white rice takes approximately an hour to cook and produces a generous three cups of fluffy cooked rice, with each grain remaining separate. Three of these recipes, Long Grain White Rice, Uncle Ben's Long Grain White Rice and Savoury Rice may be doubled, to produce about six-and-a-half cups of cooked rice. When cooled, this can be packed into serving-sized portions and frozen for future use. If doubling these recipes, increase the cooking time by 10–15 minutes.

Packaged rice has already been washed and does not require further washing. Timing is critical when cooking rice. Do not overcook the rice or it will disintegrate and stick together.

Rice pudding recipes can be found in chapter 11, 'Puddings'.

Long grain white rice

Basmati rice, sometimes called the 'king of rice', has a distinctive perfume, white colour and slimmer grain, and is particularly light and fluffy when cooked. This rice is the best one to choose for cooking in your slow cooker as it is the least sticky of all the white rices. However, other varieties of long grain white rice can be cooked effectively using this method.

1 tsp vegetable oil
1 cup (190 g) long grain white rice (preferably Basmati)
½ tsp salt
1¾ cups boiling water

SERVES 4–6

1. Preheat the slow cooker for 20 minutes.
2. Add the oil and rice and stir until each grain is coated with oil.
3. Add the salt and boiling water and stir.
4. Cover with lid and cook according to the times and settings specified, or until the liquid is absorbed and the rice is tender. If doubling the recipe, increase the cooking time by 10–15 minutes.
5. If there is any liquid left in the bottom of the slow cooker at the end of the cooking time, fluff up the rice with a fork, leave the lid off and continue to cook on high for 5–6 minutes until all the liquid evaporates.

CROCKPOT	high for approx 1 hour
SLOW COOKER	high for approx 1 hour
SPEEDY SLOW COOKER	high for 45–50 minutes

Uncle Ben's long grain white rice

Uncle Ben's long grain white rice is sometimes called 'converted' or 'parboiled' rice. Parboiling before milling forces the vitamins deeper into the grain, increasing its nutritional value. As it is already partially cooked, with some of the starch having been washed off during processing, it is less likely to break down and become sticky as a result of slow cooking.

1. Preheat the slow cooker for 20 minutes.
2. Add the oil and rice and stir until each grain is coated with oil.
3. Add the salt and boiling water and stir.
4. Cover with lid and cook according to the times and settings specified, or until the liquid is absorbed and the rice is tender. If doubling the recipe, increase the cooking time by 10–15 minutes.
5. If there is any liquid left in the bottom of the slow cooker at the end of the cooking time, fluff up the rice with a fork, leave the lid off and continue to cook on high for 5–6 minutes until all the liquid evaporates.

1 tsp vegetable oil
1 cup (190 g) Uncle Ben's long grain white rice
½ tsp salt
1⅔ cups boiling water

SERVES 4–6

CROCKPOT	**high for approx 1 hour**
SLOW COOKER	**high for approx 1 hour**
SPEEDY SLOW COOKER	**high for 45–50 minutes**

Savoury rice

1. Preheat the slow cooker for 20 minutes.
2. Add the oil and rice and stir until each grain is coated with oil.
3. Add the stock and boiling water and stir.
4. Cover with lid and cook according to the times and settings specified, or until the liquid is absorbed and the rice is tender. If doubling the recipe, increase the cooking time by 10–15 minutes.
5. If there is any liquid left in the bottom of the slow cooker at the end of the cooking time, fluff up the rice with a fork, leave the lid off and continue to cook on high for 5–6 minutes until all the liquid evaporates.

CROCKPOT	**high for approx 1 hour**
SLOW COOKER	**high for approx 1 hour**
SPEEDY SLOW COOKER	**high for 45–50 minutes**

1 tsp vegetable oil

1 cup (190 g) long grain white rice (preferably Basmati)

2 tsp powdered beef or chicken stock

1¾ cups boiling water

SERVES 4–6

Pilaf with saffron and currants

Pilaf is a delicious accompaniment to many dishes, particularly casseroles and stews. Do not overcook or the rice will become gluggy.

1. Preheat slow cooker for 20 minutes.
2. If using saffron threads, place them in a small bowl, add 1 Tbsp boiling water and leave to steep for 10 minutes.
3. Place vegetable oil, garlic, onion salt, minced ginger and lemon juice in the slow cooker and stir.
4. Add Uncle Ben's long grain white rice and hot stock to the slow cooker. Add saffron and soaking liquid, and stir.
5. Cover with lid and cook according to the times and settings specified.
6. Fifteen minutes before cooking is complete, stir in the roasted cashews and currants. Replace the lid and cook for the final quarter of an hour.
7. When it is ready, the rice will be tender and all the liquid will have been absorbed.
8. Toss with a fork when cooked, and add chopped parsley or coriander.

½ tsp saffron threads (optional)
1 Tbsp boiling water
2 tsp vegetable oil
2 cloves garlic, crushed
1 tsp onion salt
1 tsp minced ginger
1 Tbsp lemon juice
1½ cups Uncle Ben's long grain white rice, unwashed
2¾ cups chicken or vegetable stock, very hot
50 g chopped roasted cashews
¼ cup currants
3 Tbsp chopped fresh parsley or coriander

SERVES 4–6

CROCKPOT	**high for 1¼–1 hour 25 minutes**
SLOW COOKER	**high for 1 hour 10–1 hour 20 minutes**
SPEEDY SLOW COOKER	**high for 55 minutes**

Hummus with a Mediterranean Topping (see p. 58)

Vegetarian & pulses

Tips for cooking dried beans

Slow cooking is the best method to cook dried beans and lentils. No pre-soaking is required. If you prefer to soak the beans in cold water prior to cooking, the cooking times will be similar whether the beans have been soaked or not.

Cooking times will vary according to the variety, its age and quality, as well as the temperature reached in the slow cooker on high.

I don't think it is worth cooking less than 450 g of dried beans at a time, which equates to six cups of cooked beans. When the beans are cool, I set aside the amount needed and freeze the remainder in 2–3 cup lots for future use.

Red kidney beans may contain a potentially dangerous toxin which is easily destroyed by boiling for 10 minutes in a saucepan prior to cooking in the slow cooker.

Do not add salt to dried beans until they are tender, as salt will toughen the beans and prevent them cooking properly.

Cooking times for dried beans

Approximate cooking times for 450 g dried beans when cooked on high:

	Crockpot and slow cooker	**Speedy slow cooker**
Black beans	2¾–3¼hours	2¼–3hours
Black-eyed beans	2½–3 hours	2–2½ hours
Chickpeas	4–4¾ hours	3–3 ¾ hours
Dried baby lima beans	2¼–2½ hours	2–2¼ hours
Haricot beans	3¼–3½ hours	2½–2¾ hours
Red kidney beans (after parboiling)	3–3¼ hours	2½–2¾ hours

Slow cooker dried beans

This is the easiest way to cook dried beans. No overnight soaking, no parboiling (except for red kidney beans). If you are planning to use the beans in another recipe in which cooking will continue, cook them until barely tender. If you are planning to mash or purée the beans, cook until they are softer. The cooking times for dried beans are similar, whether cooked in the slow cooker or Crockpot, but faster in the 'Speedy' slow cooker. To provide extra flavour, you can add some of the optional extras suggested below.

450 g dried beans
(approx. 2¼ cups)
6 cups very hot water

optional extras
2–3 cloves garlic, crushed
1 onion, halved
bay leaves
chilli
fresh herbs

1. Preheat the slow cooker for 20 minutes.
2. Rinse beans and drain well. Place in the slow cooker and add the hot water.
3. Add optional extras to enhance flavour as desired.
4. Cover and cook according to the times and settings specified on page 50.
5. Start checking to see if the beans are cooked about 30 minutes before the suggested cooking time has been reached. The bean should be tender to the bite but still holding its shape.
6. Pour into a colander to drain.
7. Use the remaining beans in other recipes, or refrigerate or freeze them for later use.

CROCKPOT	high: see cooking times page 50
SLOW COOKER	high: see cooking times page 50
SPEEDY SLOW COOKER	high: see cooking times page 50

Bean tapenade

Tapenade is an aromatic, robust purée from Provence, consisting of olives, anchovies and capers.
I've combined these intensely flavoured ingredients with creamy lima beans to make this a milder, more subtle purée.
Lima beans are available canned, often called butter beans.
Dried lima beans can be found in health-food stores and supermarkets.

1. Drain and rinse the beans if canned.
2. Place beans in a food processor and add garlic, capers, sundried tomatoes, anchovies, olives, olive oil, lemon juice and brandy and process until smooth, scraping down the sides several times.
3. Transfer the tapenade to a serving dish and garnish with thyme.
4. Serve with pitta bread or crudités.

2 x 400 g cans butter beans or 500 g cooked dried lima beans (see directions for cooking on p. 51)
2 cloves garlic
2 Tbsp drained capers
40 g sundried tomatoes in oil, well drained
3 anchovy fillets (20 g), well drained
80 g pitted Kalamata olives
2 Tbsp olive oil
2 Tbsp lemon juice
2 Tbsp brandy
sprigs of fresh thyme for garnish

Beans with oranges and prunes

This unlikely combination of ingredients makes an unusual and delicious casserole. Serve with a salad and an interesting bread.

1. Preheat slow cooker for 20 minutes.
2. Wash and drain the beans and place in the slow cooker.
3. Add all remaining ingredients except the prunes and garnish.
4. Cover with lid and cook according to the times and settings specified.
5. Thirty minutes prior to completion of cooking, add prunes and stir.
6. Cover with lid and continue cooking for the final half hour.
7. Serve hot, garnished with fresh marjoram.

CROCKPOT	**high for 5–6 hours**
SLOW COOKER	**high for 4–5 hours**
SPEEDY SLOW COOKER	**high for 3½–4 hours**

1 cup dried black-eyed beans
2 medium carrots (200 g), peeled and diced into 1 cm cubes
200 g kumara, peeled and diced into 2 cm cubes
1 x 400 g can chopped tomatoes in juice
2 Tbsp tomato paste
½ tsp ground cinnamon
½ tsp ground nutmeg
salt and pepper
grated zest of ½ orange
4 Tbsp fresh orange juice
2 tsp dried marjoram
2½ cups hot vegetable stock
150 g pitted prunes
chopped fresh marjoram or parsley to garnish

SERVES 4–5

Black bean and parmesan salad

This visually stunning, flavoursome salad is perfect to serve with meat, chicken and fish dishes, or serve as a light meal accompanied by a good bread, or alternatively as an appetizer.

3 cups cooked dried black beans (see directions for cooking on p. 51)
1 small red capsicum, de-seeded and finely sliced
½ cup finely sliced spring onions
1 x 410 g can whole kernel corn, drained
¾ cup coarsely grated Parmesan cheese
sprigs of thyme or parsley to garnish

dressing

3 Tbsp red wine vinegar
3 Tbsp extra virgin olive oil
1 clove garlic, crushed
½ tsp prepared, chopped chilli
½ tsp raw sugar
½ tsp salt
2 Tbsp chopped fresh thyme or parsley

1. Combine black beans, red capsicum, spring onions, corn and Parmesan cheese in a bowl.
2. In a small screw-top jar shake together the dressing ingredients and pour over the salad.
3. Toss gently and tip onto a serving platter.
4. Garnish with sprigs of thyme or parsley.

SERVES 4–5 AS AN ACCOMPANIMENT

Cheesy beans

Cannellini beans (white kidney beans) are nutty and mild in flavour. During the time in the slow cooker they take on some of the other flavours in this dish: tomato, red wine, onion and garlic. The beans lose none of their bite or texture during the cooking process.
Great with a salad!

- 2 x 420 g cans cannellini beans
- 1 small onion, finely chopped
- 2 cloves garlic, crushed
- 1 x 400 g can chopped tomatoes in juice
- ¼ cup dry red wine
- ½ tsp salt
- 1½ tsp dried basil
- 1 large carrot, peeled and grated
- 2 tomatoes, skinned and diced
- 1 red capsicum, de-seeded and finely sliced
- ½ cup grated Edam cheese
- ¼ cup grated Parmesan cheese

SERVES 4–5

1. Rinse and drain the beans and place in the slow cooker.
2. Add onion, garlic, tomatoes, red wine, salt and basil and mix well.
3. Cover with lid and cook according to the times and settings specified.
4. Half an hour before cooking is complete, stir in carrot, tomatoes and capsicum. Top with the cheeses.
5. Cover with lid and cook for the final 30 minutes.
6. Serve hot.

CROCKPOT	**high for 2½–3 hours**
SLOW COOKER	**high for 2½–3 hours**
SPEEDY SLOW COOKER	**high for 2–2½ hours**

Chickpea and kumara curry

The lovely nutty flavour of chickpeas is enhanced in this richly spiced, very moreish dish.

1 Preheat the slow cooker for 20 minutes.
2 Place onion, garlic, curry powder or paste, cumin, coriander, ginger, chilli, tomato paste and chickpeas in the slow cooker. Stir well to combine.
3 Layer diced kumara over these ingredients and gently pour the boiling vegetable stock over the top, taking care that the diced kumara remains on top and that the chickpeas are submerged.
4 Cover with lid and cook according to the times and settings specified.
5 Top each serving with a spoonful of plain yoghurt and garnish with fresh basil leaves. Serve with warm naan bread.

CROCKPOT	high for 7½–8 hours
SLOW COOKER	high for 6½–7 hours
SPEEDY SLOW COOKER	high for 5–6 hours

1 large onion, finely chopped
3 cloves garlic, crushed
2–4 tsp curry powder or curry paste
½ tsp ground cumin
1 tsp ground coriander
1 Tbsp minced ginger
½ tsp prepared, chopped chilli
2 Tbsp tomato paste
200 g dried chickpeas (1 generous cup), washed and drained
700 g kumara, peeled and diced into 3 cm cubes
4¼ cups boiling vegetable stock
fresh basil leaves to garnish

SERVES 4–5

Chilli bean and chorizo casserole

The spicy flavour of dried smoked sausage blends well with beans and chilli. A lettuce and tomato salad is a good accompaniment.

1. Preheat the slow cooker for 20 minutes.
2. Place all ingredients except the red capsicum in the slow cooker.
3. Cover with lid and cook according to the times and settings specified.
4. About 30 minutes prior to serving add the red capsicum. Cover with lid and continue cooking for the final half hour.
5. Serve hot over rice or with bread to mop up the juices.

CROCKPOT	high for 9–11 hours
SLOW COOKER	high for 8–9 hours
SPEEDY SLOW COOKER	high for 7–8 hours

350 g dried pinto beans
250 g cured sausage such as chorizo, sliced 2 cm thick
2 cloves garlic, crushed
1 onion, finely chopped
1 x 400 g can diced tomatoes in juice
1 tsp prepared, chopped chilli
1 Tbsp Worcestershire sauce
1 Tbsp wine vinegar
1 tsp brown sugar
3 cups beef stock, hot
½ cup red wine
1 large red capsicum, de-seeded and finely sliced

SERVES 6

Hummus with a Mediterranean topping

Chickpeas, with their earthy, nutty flavour and firm texture, purée superbly to produce this seductive Middle Eastern appetizer. The wow factor with this particular recipe is the topping. Colourful and intensely flavoured, it is sprinkled over the hummus which is presented on a flat platter. The visual impact is stunning and the flavour superb, and the topping adds an extra dimension to an old favourite. Chickpeas are available canned (already cooked) or dried. I generally cook 450 g of dried chickpeas at a time and freeze them in single cup lots for future use.

2 cups canned or cooked dried chickpeas (see directions for cooking on p. 51)
2–3 Tbsp olive oil
2–3 cloves garlic, peeled
3 Tbsp tahini
100 ml lemon juice
¼ tsp ground cumin
salt to taste

topping

60 g sundried tomatoes in oil, drained and cut into thin strips
40 g sliced olives
60 g fetta cheese, crumbled or chopped
¼ cup chopped chives or spring onions
1 Tbsp lemon juice

1. If using canned chickpeas, rinse well and pat dry with paper towels.
2. Place chickpeas, 2 Tbsp oil, garlic, tahini, lemon juice and cumin in a food processor and purée until smooth. Taste and add salt if desired. The mixture should be thick but not stiff. Add the extra oil if necessary.
3. Spoon the hummus onto a flat platter to a depth of about 1½ cm and chill for an hour or so. Bring to room temperature for serving.
4. Combine the topping ingredients in a bowl and toss well. Scatter the topping over the hummus and serve with warm pitta bread.

Lima bean chilli dip

Nicely spicy but not too hot, these puréed beans make the perfect dip to serve with warm pitta bread. They also make an interesting filling for tacos served with sour cream, grated cheese and a tomato and shredded lettuce salad. Lima Bean Chilli Dip calls for 3 cups of cooked baby lima beans. I don't think it is worth cooking less than 450 g of dried beans at a time; this equates to 6 cups of cooked beans. I freeze half the cooked beans for future use.

1. Preheat the slow cooker for 20 minutes.
2. Place dried beans in the slow cooker and add garlic, onion, chilli, cumin, coriander and hot stock.
3. Cover with lid and cook according to the times and settings specified.
4. Remove beans from the slow cooker and drain well. Divide the beans in half and freeze half for future use. Mash the remaining beans to a chunky consistency.
5. Add avocado oil, lemon juice and chilli and mix well.
6. Allow to cool and stir in spring onion, red capsicum and sundried tomatoes. Check seasoning, adding salt if necessary.

to cook the beans

450 g dried baby lima beans, washed and drained
3 large cloves garlic, crushed
1 small onion, chopped
1 tsp prepared, chopped chilli
1 tsp ground cumin
1 tsp ground coriander
6 cups vegetable stock, hot

to assemble the dip

3 cups cooked baby lima beans
2 Tbsp avocado oil or extra virgin olive oil

7. Spoon onto a rimmed platter or a shallow, wide serving dish.
8. Top with chopped or crumbled fetta cheese and garnish with mint. Serve with warm pitta bread or crudités.

CROCKPOT	**high for 2¼–2½ hours**
SLOW COOKER	**high for 2¼–2½ hours**
SPEEDY SLOW COOKER	**high for 2–2¼ hours**

2 Tbsp lemon juice

½ tsp prepared, chopped chilli

½ cup finely chopped spring onion

½ small red capsicum, de-seeded and very finely chopped

60 g chopped sundried tomatoes in oil, well drained

salt

fetta cheese to serve

fresh mint to garnish

Mediterranean chickpea salad

Dazzling and vibrant flavours abound in this salad. The freshness of the tomatoes and spring onions, the rich oiliness of the sundried tomatoes and the saltiness of the anchovies and olives make for a taste sensation — and the perfect foil for all of these is the nutty chickpea. This salad is ideal as a light lunch for two to three people if served with an interesting bread. It is also suitable as an appetizer or accompaniment to a main course.

3 cups canned or cooked dried chickpeas (see directions for cooking on p. 51)
50 g sundried tomatoes in oil, well drained and finely sliced
½ cup pitted, sliced Kalamata olives
4–6 anchovy fillets, drained and finely chopped
½ cup thinly sliced spring onions
300 g cherry tomatoes, halved
fresh coriander leaves to garnish

dressing

3 Tbsp white wine vinegar
4 Tbsp extra virgin olive oil
1 tsp Dijon mustard
½ tsp salt
½ tsp raw sugar

1. Combine chickpeas, sundried tomatoes, olives, anchovies, spring onions and cherry tomatoes in a bowl.
2. In a small screw-top jar, shake together the dressing ingredients and pour over the salad.
3. Toss gently and tip onto a serving platter. Garnish with fresh coriander leaves.

SERVES 4 AS AN ACCOMPANIMENT

Puy lentil and vegetable casserole

Grey-green Puy lentils, with their slight earthiness and mild spicy flavour, mingle deliciously with strongly flavoured vegetables such as onions, garlic and tomatoes.

1. Place all ingredients except corn, salt and Parmesan in the slow cooker and stir to combine.
2. Cover with lid and cook according to the times and settings specified.
3. Forty-five minutes prior to completion of cooking, add the corn and stir.
4. Cover with lid and continue cooking for the final 45 minutes.
5. Check seasoning, and add salt if necessary.
6. Scatter shaved Parmesan over the top and serve piping hot.

CROCKPOT	**high for 6–7 hours**
SLOW COOKER	**high for 5–6 hours**
SPEEDY SLOW COOKER	**high for 4–4½ hours**

- 1 large onion, finely chopped
- 3 cloves garlic, crushed
- 2 medium carrots (200 g), peeled and diced into 1 cm cubes
- 250 g Puy lentils, washed and drained
- 2 red capsicums, de-seeded and sliced thickly
- 2 kumara (500 g), peeled and diced into 2 cm cubes
- 1 x 400 g can diced tomatoes in juice
- 2 Tbsp minced ginger
- 3 Tbsp sweet chilli sauce
- 3 Tbsp balsamic vinegar
- 2 cups vegetable stock
- ¾ tsp ground cinnamon
- 1½ cups whole kernel corn, canned or frozen (thawed if frozen)
- salt to taste
- shaved Parmesan cheese to serve

SERVES 4–6

Ragoût of beans and mushrooms

This is an irresistible dish, rich with mushrooms and red wine — both of which combine so well with potatoes and sour cream. It is delicious served with a green salad or green vegetable. Use a waxy potato such as Nadine so that it does not disintegrate into mush when cooked.

1. Place the dried mushrooms in a small bowl, pour the boiling water over them and leave to soak for about 30 minutes or longer.
2. Combine onion, potatoes, red kidney beans, tomato paste, red wine, ¾ cup vegetable stock, maple syrup and shiitake mushrooms and their soaking liquid in the slow cooker and mix well.
3. Cover with lid and cook according to the times and settings specified.
4. Forty minutes prior to the completion of cooking, if the ragoût looks a little dry, add the extra ¼ cup vegetable stock. Add the Portabello mushrooms and stir gently to combine.
5. Cover with lid and continue cooking for the final 40 minutes.
6. Serve topped with spoonfuls of sour cream and chopped fresh herbs.

15 g dried shiitake mushrooms
½ cup boiling water
1 large onion, finely chopped
400 g potatoes, peeled and diced into 1 cm cubes
1 x 425 g can red kidney beans, washed and drained
½ cup tomato paste
¾ cup red wine
¾ cup vegetable stock
2 Tbsp maple syrup
¼ cup vegetable stock (second measure)
220 g Portabello mushrooms, wiped and sliced
low fat sour cream to serve
¼ cup chopped fresh herbs to garnish

SERVES 4–5

CROCKPOT	**high for 6½–7 hours**
SLOW COOKER	**high for 6–6½ hours**
SPEEDY SLOW COOKER	**high for 5–5½ hours**

Smoky bean and vegetable hot pot

Smoked paprika is an exceptional spice with a truly remarkable flavour. It looks exactly like paprika — bright orangey-red in colour — but it is the smoking of the capsicum as it dries which infuses it with the most extraordinary smoky flavour.

- 1¼ cups dried baby lima beans, washed and drained
- 1 medium onion, finely chopped
- 3 cloves garlic, crushed
- 300 g kumara, peeled and diced into 3 cm cubes
- 300 g pumpkin, peeled, de-seeded and diced into 3 cm cubes
- 2 large red capsicums, de-seeded and sliced thickly
- 3½ cups vegetable stock, hot
- ½ cup tomato paste
- ½–1 tsp prepared, chopped chilli
- 1½ tsp sweet smoked paprika
- ¼ cup chopped fresh herbs to garnish
- 150 g sour cream or Greek yoghurt to serve

SERVES 5

1. Preheat the slow cooker for 20 minutes.
2. Place beans in the slow cooker.
3. Add all the remaining ingredients except herbs, sour cream and yoghurt.
4. Cover with the lid and cook according to the times and settings specified.
5. Sprinkle with chopped herbs and serve topped with spoonfuls of sour cream or yoghurt, and accompanied by rice or crusty bread and a salad.

CROCKPOT	**high for 5–6 hours**
SLOW COOKER	**high for 4¾–5¼ hours**
SPEEDY SLOW COOKER	**high for 3¾–4½ hours**

Spicy chickpea and vegetable chilli

Chunky, robust and brimming with vegetables — delicious, filling fare.

1. Wash chickpeas and drain well. Place in the slow cooker and add onion, capsicums, courgettes, kumara, basil, cumin, salt and pepper.
2. In a small bowl combine tomatoes, tomato paste and chilli, and mix well.
3. Pour into the slow cooker and stir the contents to combine.
4. Cover with lid and cook according to the times and settings specified.
5. Stir in lemon juice and adjust seasoning to taste.
6. Serve hot, garnished with a dollop of sour cream and a sprinkling of cheese.
7. Serve remaining sour cream and grated cheese in a bowl alongside.

CROCKPOT	high for 4–5 hours
SLOW COOKER	high for 3¾–4½ hours
SPEEDY SLOW COOKER	high for 3¼–3½ hours

2 x 300 g cans chickpeas or 2½ cups cooked chickpeas
1 small onion, finely chopped
2 large red capsicums, de-seeded and sliced thickly
3 medium courgettes, cut into 2 cm slices
400 g kumara, peeled and diced into 1 cm cubes
2 tsp dried basil
1 tsp ground cumin
½ tsp salt
freshly ground black pepper
1 x 400 g can diced tomatoes in juice
2 Tbsp tomato paste
1 tsp prepared, chopped chilli
2 Tbsp lemon juice
1 cup sour cream to serve
1 cup grated tasty or Parmesan cheese to serve

SERVES 4–5

Spicy potatoes with yellow split peas

This is real comfort food. The split peas disintegrate into a purée, and the potato chunks absorb the aromatic spices and become tender. Use a waxy potato such as Nadine so that the pieces stay intact. Serve with a crisp salad and rice or naan bread and offer side dishes as you would for any curry.

1. Preheat the slow cooker for 20 minutes.
2. Put oil in the slow cooker and, using a pastry brush, brush it over the sides and base of the slow cooker.
3. Add onion and split peas and stir.
4. Add the potatoes, spreading them evenly over the onions and split peas.
5. In a bowl combine the cumin, ginger, turmeric, curry powder and hot stock.
6. Gently pour hot stock over the potatoes making sure all of the potatoes are coated with the stock.
7. Cover with lid and cook according to the times and settings specified. Taste and add salt if necessary.
8. About 5 minutes before serving stir in the spinach. It will wilt and soften almost immediately.
9. Scatter torn mint leaves over the top and serve.

CROCKPOT	high for 5½–6 hours
SLOW COOKER	high for 4¾–5¼ hours
SPEEDY SLOW COOKER	high for 3½–4 hours

2 tsp canola oil
1 red onion, finely chopped
1½ cups yellow split peas, washed and drained
800 g waxy potatoes, peeled and diced into 2–3 cm cubes
1 tsp each ground cumin, ground ginger and ground turmeric
1–2 Tbsp mild curry powder
4 cups boiling vegetable stock
150 g approx. baby spinach leaves or larger leaves, chopped
salt
fresh mint leaves to garnish

SERVES 4–6

Sunny brunch eggs with brie

This jazzed-up version of baked eggs makes a special breakfast or brunch. Six or eight individual ramekins will fit into a slow cooker. If they will not all fit on the base, arrange the dishes so that two or three are balanced on the ones below.

for one portion

1 Tbsp finely chopped sundried tomatoes in oil, well drained

2 eggs

1 Tbsp chopped chives or parsley

3–4 very thin slices of Brie

salt and freshly ground black pepper to taste

SERVES 1

1. Preheat the slow cooker for 20 minutes.
2. For each serving, place sundried tomatoes in a 7–8 cm ramekin.
3. Break the eggs on top, sprinkle with chives or parsley and cover with slices of Brie.
4. Sprinkle with salt and pepper.
5. Arrange the ramekins to fit on the base of the slow cooker.
6. Pour in boiling water to halfway up the sides of the bottom layer of ramekins.
7. Cover with lid and cook according to the times and settings specified.
8. Serve immediately.

CROCKPOT	**high for 45–55 minutes**
SLOW COOKER	**high for 40–50 minutes**
SPEEDY SLOW COOKER	**high for 35–40 minutes**

Chilli vegetables with coconut

This is a pretty dish — golden yellow and very fragrant. The vegetables and spices cook gently together in the creamy coconut milk, which is thickened slightly towards the end of the cooking time by the addition of ground almonds. Serve with crusty bread and a salad.

1. Place onion, garlic, pumpkin, potatoes, carrots and tomatoes in the slow cooker.
2. In a bowl mix together the chilli, ginger, cumin, paprika, brown sugar and coconut milk. Add to the slow cooker and stir well to combine all the ingredients.
3. Cover with lid and cook following the times and settings specified until the vegetables are tender.
4. About 30 minutes before serving, stir in the ground almonds.
5. Check seasoning, adding salt if necessary.
6. Cover with lid and continue cooking for the remaining 30 minutes.
7. Sprinkle with the slivered almonds and serve.

CROCKPOT	**high for 6–6½ hours**
SLOW COOKER	**high for 5½–6 hours**
SPEEDY SLOW COOKER	**high for 4½–5 hours**

1 small red onion, diced finely
3 cloves garlic, crushed
600 g peeled, de-seeded pumpkin, diced into 3 cm cubes
2 medium potatoes (300 g), peeled and diced into 2–3 cm cubes
2 medium carrots (200 g), diced finely
1 x 400 g can diced tomatoes in juice
½–1 tsp prepared chopped chilli
1 tsp each ground ginger, ground cumin, sweet smoked paprika and brown sugar
1 x 400ml can light coconut milk
3 Tbsp ground almonds
salt to taste
½ cup toasted slivered almonds to garnish

SERVES 5–6

Cheese and egg bake

This savoury bread and cheese pudding is a great dish to serve for brunch or a light Sunday evening meal. Serve with rashers of crispy fried bacon or a salad, depending on the time of day. Choose a good quality white bread — a sour dough bread is perfect for this dish.

non-stick cooking spray
5–6 thick slices of white bread with crusts removed (120 g), cut into 2 cm squares
70 g tasty cheese, grated
4 eggs, size 7
1½ cups standard milk
2 tsp Dijon mustard
3 Tbsp fresh basil pesto
½ tsp salt
⅛ tsp cayenne pepper
½ tsp paprika
2 Tbsp grated Parmesan cheese

SERVES 4

1. Preheat the slow cooker for 20 minutes.
2. Place trivet inside slow cooker. (Three $2 coins work well.)
3. Using non-stick cooking spray, spray the base and sides of a 5-cup capacity casserole or baking dish which will fit inside the slow cooker.
4. Place half the bread in the casserole dish and sprinkle with half the grated cheese. Top with remaining bread and then remaining cheese.
5. In a medium-sized bowl, beat together eggs, milk, mustard, pesto, salt and cayenne pepper.
6. Pour this evenly over the bread and cheese mixture, gently pushing the pieces of bread down beneath the egg and milk mixture.
7. Combine paprika and Parmesan cheese and sprinkle over the top. Do not cover.
8. Using a foil strap (see p. 11), lift the casserole dish onto the trivet in the slow cooker. Pour warm water into the slow cooker to come halfway up the sides of the casserole dish.

9 Cover with lid and cook according to the times and settings specified. When cooked, the centre of the bake should feel firm and spring back when touched.

10 Lift from the slow cooker. Allow to rest for 5–10 minutes and serve.

CROCKPOT	**low for 3¼–3½ hours**
SLOW COOKER	**low for 3–3¼ hours**
SPEEDY SLOW COOKER	**high for 2¼–2½ hours**

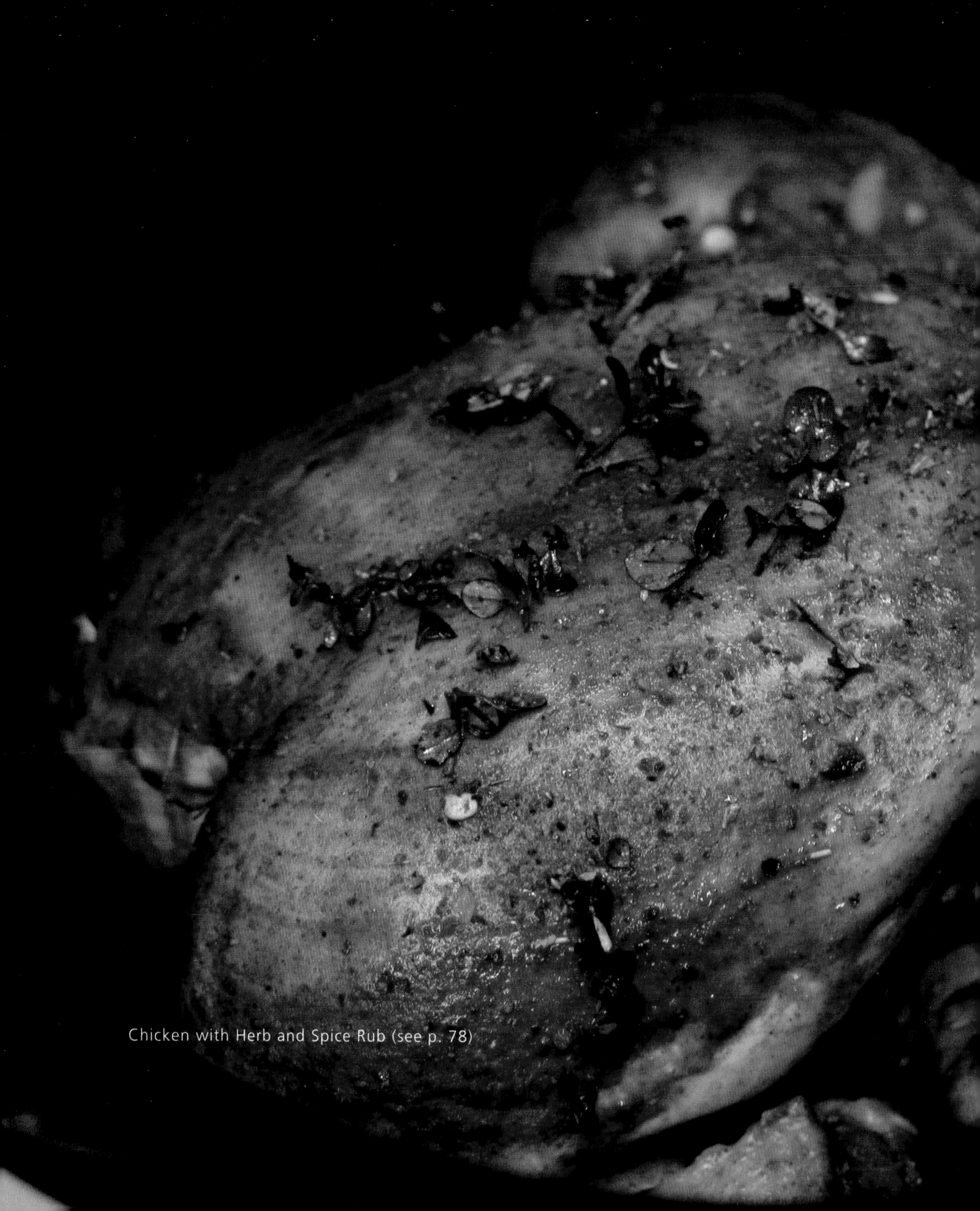

Chicken with Herb and Spice Rub (see p. 78)

Chicken

Chicken cooked in the slow cooker is the best chicken I have ever eaten. A whole chicken can be cooked without pre-browning or the addition of any liquid. It emerges moist and tender.

Chicken pieces may be pre-browned in a frying pan to eliminate excess fat but I prefer to remove the skin from the chicken pieces and place the chicken straight into the slow cooker.

The different types of bone-in-chicken portions are interchangeable in the following recipes because their cooking times are similar. Use whichever you have on hand: chicken pieces, drumsticks, legs or 'semi-boned' thighs.

Root vegetables and onions will take longer to cook than the chicken. When cooking chicken dishes that contain these vegetables, chop the onions very finely and dice the root vegetables into 1–2 cm cubes. Place onions and vegetables at the bottom or sides of the slow cooker and arrange the chicken on top.

The vegetables will be submerged in liquid and will cook more quickly and evenly.

Slow cooker whole chicken

Slow cooking is a great way to cook a whole chicken. It emerges tender and moist and no tending is required — a boon for the busy cook. Although the chicken won't be browned, you can choose from several different coatings to give it colour and extra flavour.

Once the chicken is cooked it can be lifted from the slow cooker, carved and served hot with some of the delicious cooking juices spooned over the top. Alternatively you can thicken the cooking juices to serve as a gravy.

The cooked chicken may also be cooled and jointed, sliced or shredded for use in recipes calling for cooked chicken.

For best results remove as much skin and fat as possible from the chicken prior to cooking. The cooking juices will then be almost completely fat free and delicious served with the chicken.

It is not necessary to add liquid to the slow cooker when cooking a whole chicken. Moisture inside the crockpot forms a vapour seal between the lid and the bowl which stops steam escaping. Because of this, a cup or more of liquid usually accumulates in the slow cooker during cooking.

Flavourings

Here are several ways to vary the flavour of a whole chicken. Choose one or more of the following flavourings to go into the chicken cavity:

Garlic: four or five peeled cloves of garlic, crushed with the blade of a knife;
Herbs: a handful of fresh herbs: sprigs of tarragon are especially good;
Citrus: a lemon or an orange cut into quarters;
Onion: one medium onion, roughly chopped.

Once the chicken is cooked

Lift the chicken from the slow cooker. (Don't leave cooked chicken in the slow cooker.) If serving hot, carve and spoon some of the delicious juices over the top.

If the chicken is to be served cold or in a recipe calling for cooked chicken, cover the chicken and refrigerate until required.

Making the gravy

If you want to thicken the juices to make a gravy or sauce, pour the juices into a small saucepan. In a small bowl, mix 1½ tablespoons of cornflour with 2 tablespoons of brandy, water, chicken stock or wine until smooth, and stir into the liquid in the saucepan. Bring to the boil, stirring constantly, then reduce the heat and simmer for a couple of minutes until the sauce thickens.

A tablespoon of redcurrant, cranberry or apple jelly can be stirred into the gravy to give a lovely flavour boost.

If the juices which have accumulated in the slow cooker are not being served with the chicken, pour into suitable containers and freeze. This is a very flavoursome stock, ideal for adding to soups and casseroles later.

Chicken with herb and spice rub

The rub is an aromatic mixture of dried herbs and spices, all of which have an affinity with chicken.

1 large whole chicken, about 2 kg, and choice of flavouring (p. 77)
1–2 tsp olive or canola oil
2 tsp flour
2 tsp paprika
2 tsp curry powder
2 tsp dried basil
2 tsp dried oregano
1 tsp onion salt

SERVES 4–6

1. Remove skin from chicken and pat chicken dry with paper towels.
2. Fill chicken cavity with one of the suggested flavourings (p. 77) — fresh herbs, orange quarters, or a combination of both are really delicious.
3. Rub chicken all over with oil and place in the slow cooker, breast-side down.
4. Combine flour, paprika, curry powder, basil, oregano and onion salt, and mix well.
5. Sprinkle about half of the mixture over the chicken, and pat it on evenly.
6. Turn the chicken over and sprinkle the remaining mixture over the chicken, patting to coat chicken evenly. Leave chicken breast-side up to cook.
7. Cover with lid and cook according to the times and settings specified.
8. Serve with the cooking juices spooned over the chicken or make gravy (see p. 77).

CROCKPOT	**low for 7–8 hours, high for 3½–4 hours**
SLOW COOKER	**low for 6–7 hours, high for 3–3½ hours**
SPEEDY SLOW COOKER	**low for 4–4½ hours high for 3–3½ hours**

Chicken with maple and mustard

These wonderfully aromatic ingredients are superb with the mild flavour of chicken.

1 large whole chicken, about 2 kg, and choice of flavouring (p. 77)
2 Tbsp maple syrup
2 Tbsp wholegrain mustard
2 cloves garlic, crushed
1 Tbsp minced ginger

SERVES 4–6

1. Remove skin from chicken and pat chicken dry with paper towels.
2. Fill chicken cavity with one of the suggested flavourings (p. 77) — the quartered lemon is a good choice for this recipe.
3. Place chicken in the slow cooker breast-side down.
4. Combine remaining ingredients in a small bowl and mix until smooth.
5. Brush about half of the paste over the upper side of the chicken, using a pastry brush.
6. Turn the chicken over and brush with the remaining paste, coating evenly. Leave the chicken breast-side up to cook.
7. Cover with lid and cook according to the times and settings specified.
8. Serve with the cooking juices spooned over the top, or make gravy (see p. 77).

CROCKPOT	**low for 7–8 hours, high for 3½–4 hours**
SLOW COOKER	**low for 6–7 hours, high for 3–3½ hours**
SPEEDY SLOW COOKER	**low for 4–4½ hours high for 3–3½ hours**

Chinese red chicken

In Chinese cuisine, chicken is sometimes braised in a reddish-brown sauce hence 'red cooked'. Hoisin sauce is a spicy, sweet sauce made from soya beans, garlic, chillies and various spices. It is used as both a condiment and an ingredient in Chinese cooking, and is available in supermarkets.

1 whole large chicken, about 2 kg, and choice of flavouring (p. 77)
3 Tbsp dark soy sauce
1 Tbsp honey
1 Tbsp minced ginger
½ tsp ground cinnamon
½ tsp Chinese five spice
1 Tbsp Hoisin sauce

SERVES 4–6

1. Remove skin from chicken and pat chicken dry with paper towels.
2. Fill chicken cavity with one of the suggested flavourings (p. 77). The cloves of garlic and chopped onion are both delicious for this dish — or else use both onion and garlic together.
3. Place chicken in the slow cooker breast-side down.
4. Combine all remaining ingredients in a small bowl and mix until smooth.
5. Brush about half the paste over the upper side of the chicken using a pastry brush.
6. Turn chicken over and brush with remaining paste, coating evenly. Leave chicken breast-side up to cook.
7. Cover with lid and cook according to the times and settings specified.
8. Serve with the cooking juices spooned over the chicken, or make gravy (see p. 77).

CROCKPOT	**low for 7–8 hours, high for 3½–4 hours**
SLOW COOKER	**low for 6–7 hours, high for 3–3½ hours**
SPEEDY SLOW COOKER	**low for 4–4½ hours high for 3–3½ hours**

Devilled chicken

This spicy sauce adds exciting flavour and colour to the chicken.

1 large whole chicken, about 2 kg, and choice of flavouring (p. 77)
2 Tbsp brown sugar
1 tsp ground ginger
1 tsp dry mustard
⅛–¼ tsp cayenne pepper
2 Tbsp tomato paste
2 Tbsp Worcestershire sauce
2 Tbsp balsamic vinegar

SERVES 4–6

1. Remove skin from chicken and pat the chicken dry with paper towels.
2. Fill chicken cavity with one of the suggested flavourings (p. 77). I often use the cloves of garlic for this recipe.
3. Place chicken in the slow cooker breast-side down.
4. Combine all remaining ingredients in a small bowl and mix until smooth.
5. Brush about half the paste over the upper side of the chicken, using a pastry brush.
6. Turn chicken over and brush other side with the remaining paste, coating chicken evenly. Leave chicken breast-side up to cook.
7. Cover with lid and cook according to the times and settings specified.
8. Serve with the cooking juices spooned over the chicken, or make gravy (see p. 77).

CROCKPOT	**low for 7–8 hours, high for 3½–4 hours**
SLOW COOKER	**low for 6–7 hours, high for 3–3½ hours**
SPEEDY SLOW COOKER	**low for 4–4½ hours high for 3–3½ hours**

Sundried tomato glazed chicken

Here a whole chicken is brushed with a zesty tomato and orange glaze, flavouring the chicken as it cooks and keeping it succulently tender.

1 large whole chicken, about 2 kg
1 orange
1 Tbsp brown sugar
2 Tbsp minced ginger
2 cloves garlic, crushed
2 Tbsp balsamic vinegar
3 Tbsp tomato paste
40 g sundried tomatoes in oil, well drained and finely chopped

SERVES 4–6

1. Remove skin from chicken, and pat chicken dry with paper towels.
2. Grate zest from orange. Place grated zest in a small bowl and set aside. Cut orange into quarters and place inside the chicken cavity and close with toothpicks.
3. Place chicken in the slow cooker breast-side down.
4. Combine brown sugar, ginger, garlic, balsamic vinegar, tomato paste and chopped sundried tomatoes with orange zest. Mix well.
5. Brush about half of this paste over the upper side of the chicken, using a pastry brush.
6. Turn chicken over and brush with remaining paste, coating evenly. Leave chicken breast-side up to cook.
7. Cover with lid and cook according to the times and settings specified.
8. Serve with the cooking juices spooned over the chicken, or thicken juices to make gravy (see p. 77).

CROCKPOT	**low for 7–8 hours, high for 3½–4 hours**
SLOW COOKER	**low for 6–7 hours, high for 3–3½ hours**
SPEEDY SLOW COOKER	**low for 4–4½ hours high for 3–3½ hours**

Chicken and bacon casserole

Chicken and bacon is a delicious combination, and in this robust casserole, the tomatoes and mushrooms complement them well.

1. Remove skin from chicken.
2. Toss chicken with flour in a plastic bag. Shake off any excess.
3. Combine bacon and onion and place in the slow cooker. Arrange chicken on top.
4. In a small bowl combine mustard, tomatoes, tomato paste, chicken stock or wine, marjoram and basil. Stir well and spoon over the chicken.
5. Cover with lid and cook according to the times and settings specified.
6. Thirty minutes before the cooking time is complete, turn the control to high (if cooking on low).
7. Add mushrooms and stir gently to distribute.
8. Cover with lid and cook for the final half hour.
9. Serve garnished with chopped marjoram.

6–8 large chicken drumsticks
3 Tbsp flour
3–4 rashers bacon, trimmed and chopped
1 onion, finely chopped
1 Tbsp wholegrain mustard
1 x 400 g can diced tomatoes in juice
3 Tbsp tomato paste
¼ cup chicken stock or wine (red or white)
1 tsp dried marjoram
1 tsp dried basil
150 g button mushrooms, wiped and sliced
chopped fresh marjoram to garnish

CROCKPOT	**low for 7–8 hours, high for 3½–4½ hours**
SLOW COOKER	**low for 6–7 hours, high for 3–4 hours**
SPEEDY SLOW COOKER	**low for 4½–5 hours high for 3–3½ hours**

SERVES 4–6

Chicken and cranberry casserole

This is a special chicken dish that combines the complementary flavours of garlic, orange and tomato with the sweet tang of cranberries. If the cranberries are added at the beginning, they make the sauce too sweet and much of their attractive taste, shape and colour is lost.

- 7–8 boneless, skinless chicken thighs (about 1 kg)
- 3 Tbsp flour
- 3 cloves garlic, crushed
- 1 tsp onion salt
- ¼ tsp ground cloves
- zest of one orange
- 3 Tbsp tomato paste
- 3 Tbsp marmalade
- ¼ cup lemon juice
- ½ cup chicken stock
- ⅓ cup dried cranberries
- fresh mint to garnish

SERVES 5–6

1. Toss chicken with flour in a plastic bag. Shake off any excess.
2. Place garlic, onion salt, cloves, orange zest, tomato paste, marmalade, lemon juice and chicken stock in the slow cooker and stir to mix.
3. Place chicken in the sauce, turning so that all sides are coated.
4. Cover with lid and cook according to the times and settings specified.
5. Thirty minutes prior to serving, stir in cranberries.
6. Cover with lid and cook for the final half hour.
7. Garnish with mint sprigs. Serve with couscous or rice accompanied by a green vegetable or salad.

CROCKPOT	**low for 6–7 hours, high for 3½–4 hours**
SLOW COOKER	**low for 5–6 hours, high for 3–3½ hours**
SPEEDY SLOW COOKER	**low for 3½–4 hours high, for 2¾–3 hours**

Chicken hot pot

Chicken and vegetables simmer slowly in this mild mustard and herb sauce. The bacon adds flavour and keeps the chicken moist.

1. Trim chicken of excess fat.
2. Toss potato and pumpkin with flour in a plastic bag. Tip into the slow cooker.
3. Sprinkle onion salt and thyme over the vegetables.
4. Wrap a bacon rasher around each piece of chicken and arrange chicken on top of the vegetables in the slow cooker.
5. In a small bowl combine chicken stock, Dijon mustard and tomato paste. Spoon this evenly over the chicken.
6. Cover with lid and cook according to the times and settings specified.
7. Garnish with fresh thyme, and serve with a green vegetable and crusty bread to mop up the juices.

6 chicken thighs, semi-boned and skinless (1 kg)
450 g potatoes, peeled and diced into 2 cm cubes
450 g pumpkin, peeled, de-seeded and diced into 3 cm cubes
3 Tbsp flour
½ tsp onion salt
1½ tsp dried thyme
6 rashers streaky bacon
¾ cup chicken stock
1½ Tbsp Dijon mustard
1½ Tbsp tomato paste
chopped fresh thyme to garnish

SERVES 6

CROCKPOT	**low for 8½–10 hours, high for 4¾–5½ hours**
SLOW COOKER	**low for 8–10 hours, high for 4–5 hours**
SPEEDY SLOW COOKER	**low for 6–7 hours high for 3–3½ hours**

Chicken paprika

Paprika with its mild, sweet flavour enhances this rich tomato sauce which is quick to make and tastes extremely good. Serve with fluffy mashed potatoes or over noodles.

1. Trim chicken of excess fat.
2. Toss chicken with flour in a plastic bag. Shake off any excess.
3. Combine tomatoes, garlic, paprika, onion salt, tomato paste, brown sugar and chicken stock or wine in the slow cooker.
4. Place chicken in this mixture and turn to coat evenly.
5. Cover with lid and cook according to the times and settings specified.
6. Thirty minutes before the cooking time is complete, turn the control to high (if cooking on low). Add the capsicum and stir gently to distribute. Cover with lid and continue cooking for the final half hour.
7. Serve the chicken, topping each serving with a spoonful of sour cream and a sprinkling of parsley.

CROCKPOT	**low for 7–8 hours, high for 3½–4 hours**
SLOW COOKER	**low for 6–7 hours, high for 3–3½ hours**
SPEEDY SLOW COOKER	**low for 4½–5 hours high for 2¾–3 hours**

6 chicken thighs, semi-boned and skinless (about 1 kg)
2 Tbsp flour
1 x 400 g can diced tomatoes in juice
2 cloves garlic crushed
4 tsp paprika
¾ tsp onion salt
2 Tbsp tomato paste
2 tsp brown sugar
⅓ cup chicken stock or red wine
1 red capsicum, de-seeded and finely sliced
⅓ cup low fat sour cream to serve
2 Tbsp chopped parsley to garnish

SERVES 4–6

Chicken peanut curry

Peanut butter adds a delicious richness and depth of flavour to this mild and fragrant chicken curry.

1. Turn the slow cooker to the setting you intend to cook on.
2. Trim excess fat from chicken. Cut chicken thighs in half and toss with flour in a plastic bag. Shake off any excess.
3. Combine peanut butter, sweet chilli sauce, soy sauce, lemon juice, curry powder, paprika, coriander and ginger in the slow cooker and stir to mix. As the slow cooker heats up, the peanut butter will soften and all the sauce ingredients can be mixed together smoothly.
4. Add the chicken stock and stir well.
5. Add the chicken and stir to combine.
6. Cover with lid and cook according to the times and settings specified.
7. Serve over rice or couscous, garnished with coriander or parsley.

6 boneless, skinless chicken thighs (1 kg)
3 Tbsp flour
¼ cup peanut butter
2 Tbsp sweet chilli sauce
2 Tbsp soy sauce
2 Tbsp lemon juice
2 tsp mild curry powder
2 tsp paprika
1 tsp ground coriander
1 Tbsp minced ginger
½ cup chicken stock
fresh coriander or parsley, chopped

SERVES 4–6

CROCKPOT	**low for 5–6 hours, high for 3–3½ hours**
SLOW COOKER	**low for 4½–5½ hours, high for 2½–3 hours**
SPEEDY SLOW COOKER	**low for 2¾–3 hours high for 2–2¼ hours**

Chicken tagine with prunes and apricots

Spices, honey and dried fruits impart their sweet and sour flavours to this wonderfully aromatic, slowly simmered stew — so evocative of Arabian cooking.

1. Trim excess fat from chicken.
2. In a small bowl place saffron threads in hot chicken stock. Add honey and garlic and leave to steep for 10–15 minutes.
3. Toss chicken with flour in a plastic bag, shaking off any excess. Arrange chicken in the slow cooker.
4. Add cayenne pepper, coriander, cinnamon and onion salt to the bowl containing the saffron and chicken stock mixture and stir to combine.
5. Pour this mixture evenly over the chicken.
6. Cover with lid and cook according to the times and settings specified.
7. Thirty minutes before cooking time is complete, turn the control to high (if cooking on low).
8. Add prunes and apricots, stirring gently.
9. Cover with lid and cook for the final half hour.
10. Garnish with coriander or parsley, and serve over couscous.

8 boneless, skinless chicken thighs
½ tsp saffron threads
⅔ cup chicken stock, hot
2 Tbsp honey
3 cloves garlic, crushed
2 Tbsp plain flour
¼ tsp cayenne pepper
1 tsp ground coriander
1 tsp ground cinnamon
1 tsp onion salt
100 g pitted prunes
80 g Central Otago dried apricots, halved
chopped fresh coriander or parsley to garnish

SERVES 6

CROCKPOT	**low for 6½–8 hours, high for 3½–4 hours**
SLOW COOKER	**low for 6–7 hours, high for 3–3½ hours**
SPEEDY SLOW COOKER	**low for 4–5 hours high for 2¾–3 hours**

Chilli chicken and kumara

Here the chicken is cooked in a sauce of richly spiced coconut milk on a bed of kumara. Serve with rice or creamy mashed potatoes, and a simple salad or some lightly cooked green vegetables.

- 6–8 large chicken drumsticks (1 kg)
- 750 g golden kumara
- ½ tsp chopped, prepared chilli
- 3 Tbsp sweet chilli sauce
- 3 Tbsp peanut butter, warmed
- 2 Tbsp fish sauce
- 1 Tbsp white wine vinegar
- 1 x 400 g can diced tomatoes in juice
- ¾ cup light coconut milk or light coconut cream
- 1–2 Tbsp chopped fresh coriander or mint to garnish

SERVES 6

1. Remove skin and excess fat from chicken.
2. Peel and thinly slice kumara (½ cm thick) and arrange in layers on the base of the slow cooker.
3. In a medium-sized bowl combine chilli, sweet chilli sauce, peanut butter, fish sauce and vinegar and mix until smooth.
4. Add tomatoes and coconut milk or light coconut cream and stir to combine.
5. Place chicken on top of the kumara and spoon the sauce over the top.
6. Cover with lid and cook according to the times and settings specified.
7. Sprinkle with chopped coriander or mint and serve.

CROCKPOT	**low for 8½–10 hours, high for 4–4½ hours**
SLOW COOKER	**low for 8–10 hours, high for 3½–4 hours**
SPEEDY SLOW COOKER	**low for 5½–6½ hours high for 2¾–3 hours**

Crockpot barbecued chicken

Children particularly love this spicy combination and it is another super-quick idea for busy days.

1. Trim chicken of excess fat.
2. Toss chicken with flour in a plastic bag. Shake off any excess.
3. Add remaining ingredients except the parsley to the slow cooker and stir to mix.
4. Place chicken in the sauce, turning so that all sides are coated.
5. Cover and cook according to the times and settings specified.
6. Sprinkle with chopped fresh parsley and serve with a good crusty bread to soak up the juices.

CROCKPOT	**low for 5–6 hours, high for 3–3½ hours**
SLOW COOKER	**low for 4½–5½ hours, high for 2½–3 hours**
SPEEDY SLOW COOKER	**low for 2¾–3 hours high for 2–2¼ hours**

6 chicken thighs, semi-boned and skinless (about 1 kg)
3 Tbsp flour
3 Tbsp tomato sauce (ketchup)
2 Tbsp red wine vinegar
1 tsp brown sugar
1 Tbsp Worcestershire sauce
1 tsp smoked paprika
¼ tsp prepared, chopped chilli
½ cup chicken stock
fresh parsley to garnish

SERVES 4–6

Honey mustard glazed chicken

Piquant and tangy, this is so quick to assemble and a great favourite with everybody. Serve with a simple salad and a good bread.

6 chicken thighs, semi-boned and skinless (about 1 kg)
3 Tbsp flour
1 Tbsp Dijon mustard
2 Tbsp honey
1 Tbsp soy sauce
½ tsp prepared, chopped chilli
2 cloves garlic, crushed
2 Tbsp tomato paste
¾ cup chicken stock

SERVES 4–6

1. Turn the slow cooker to the setting you intend to cook on.
2. Trim excess fat from chicken and toss with flour in a plastic bag. Shake off any excess.
3. Combine remaining ingredients in the slow cooker. As the slow cooker warms, the honey and mustard will soften and the sauce ingredients can be stirred to combine.
4. Add chicken and stir gently so that all sides are coated in the sauce.
5. Cover with lid and cook according to the times and settings specified.
6. Serve with the cooking juices spooned over the chicken.

CROCKPOT	**low for 5–6 hours, high for 3–3½ hours**
SLOW COOKER	**low for 4½–5½ hours, high for 2½–3 hours**
SPEEDY SLOW COOKER	**low for 2¾–3 hours high for 2–2¼ hours**

Peachy chicken

The combination of chicken with peaches is delicious and gives this dish a light, summery flavour.

6 large chicken thighs, semi-boned and skinless (about 1 kg)
3 Tbsp flour
1 x 400 g can sliced peaches in juice
3 cloves garlic, crushed
1 tsp ground ginger
½ tsp ground cinnamon
⅛ tsp cayenne pepper
1 tsp paprika
2 tsp brown sugar
2 Tbsp red wine vinegar
¼ cup red wine or chicken stock
toasted slivered almonds to garnish

SERVES 4–6

1. Trim excess fat from chicken and toss chicken in the flour in a plastic bag. Shake off any excess.
2. Measure ⅓ cup peach juice and place it in the slow cooker. Drain peaches and set aside.
3. Add garlic, ginger, cinnamon, cayenne pepper, paprika, brown sugar, red wine vinegar and red wine or chicken stock to the slow cooker. Stir until smooth and well mixed.
4. Place chicken in this sauce, turning so all sides are coated. Cover with lid and cook according to the times and settings specified.
5. Thirty minutes prior to the end of the cooking, turn the slow cooker to high (if cooking on low). Turn the chicken pieces over, add peaches and stir gently so they are evenly distributed throughout the sauce.
6. Cover with lid and cook for the final half hour.
7. Serve sprinkled with slivered almonds.

CROCKPOT	**low for 6½–7 hours, high for 3½–4 hours**
SLOW COOKER	**low for 5½–6½ hours, high for 3–3½ hours**
SPEEDY SLOW COOKER	**low for 3–3½ hours, high for 2¾–3 hours**

Red curry chicken

This is an aromatic rather than a hot curry — mild with rich, creamy juices. Serve it with rice or mashed potato and a green vegetable, or simply with a salad and a good bread. Red curry paste with its wonderfully complex flavours is made from red chillies, garlic, lemon grass, ginger and coriander and is available from the supermarket.

6–8 large chicken thighs or drums, bone in (1–1.2 kg)
3 Tbsp plain flour
1 Tbsp brown sugar
2–4 tsp red curry paste
1 Tbsp dark soy sauce
2 Tbsp tomato paste
2 Tbsp fish sauce
1 x 400 g can light coconut milk or light coconut cream
1 x 300 g can whole kernel corn, drained
2 Tbsp lemon juice
½ cup finely sliced spring onions

1. Remove skin from chicken and place chicken in the slow cooker.
2. Combine flour, brown sugar, red curry paste, soy sauce, tomato paste and fish sauce in a bowl and mix well. Add the coconut milk or cream and stir to combine.
3. Spoon this mixture over chicken in the slow cooker.
4. Cover with lid and cook according to the times and settings specified.
5. Thirty minutes before completion of cooking, turn the control to high (if cooking on low) and stir in the corn and lemon juice.
6. Cover with lid and continue cooking for the final half hour.
7. Stir in the spring onions and serve.

SERVES 6

CROCKPOT	**low for 7–8 hours, high for 3½–4 hours**
SLOW COOKER	**low for 6–7½ hours, high for 3–3½ hours**
SPEEDY SLOW COOKER	**low for 4–5 hours, high for 2¾–3 hours**

Sweet and sour chicken

This is an extremely easy and useful dish with delicious sweet and sour juices. For those days when time is precious, simply assemble these ingredients in the slow cooker, turn it on and forget it.

- 6 chicken thighs, semi-boned and skinless, (about 1 kg)
- 3 Tbsp flour
- 1½ tsp ground ginger
- 1 Tbsp sugar
- 2 Tbsp white wine vinegar
- 1/8 tsp cayenne pepper
- 1 x 32 g packet onion soup mix
- 1 x 440 g can pineapple pieces in juice
- 1 red capsicum, deseeded and finely sliced
- 1–2 spring onions, trimmed and cut finely on the diagonal

1. Trim the chicken of any excess fat. Toss chicken with flour in a plastic bag, shaking off any excess.
2. Place ground ginger, sugar, white wine vinegar, cayenne pepper and the onion soup mix in the slow cooker and stir to combine.
3. Gradually add pineapple juice and stir until well mixed.
4. Place the chicken pieces in the slow cooker and turn the chicken pieces to coat evenly with the sauce.
5. Add pineapple pieces and sliced capsicum to the slow cooker and stir to combine.
6. Cover with lid and cook according to the times and settings specified.
7. Mix in the spring onions and serve over rice.

CROCKPOT low for 7–8 hours, high for 3–4 hours

SLOW COOKER low for 6–7 hours, high for 3–3½ hours

SPEEDY SLOW COOKER low for 3 ¾–4¼ hours high for 2½–2¾ hours

SERVES 4–6

Tandoori chicken and chickpeas

Mildly spicy but not too hot, this dish is popular with both children and adults. The simple, fragrant sauce coating the chicken is quickly assembled from store cupboard ingredients. Serve with naan or pitta bread and a salad.

6 large chicken thighs, semi-boned and skinless (about 1 kg)
3 Tbsp flour
2 tsp paprika
2 tsp mild curry powder
⅛–¼ tsp cayenne pepper
2 tsp minced ginger
1 Tbsp brown sugar
1 Tbsp tomato paste
⅓ cup chicken stock
3 Tbsp lemon juice
1 x 400 g can chickpeas or 1–1½ cups cooked chickpeas
thick, creamy yoghurt to serve
torn mint leaves to garnish

SERVES 4–6

1. Trim chicken of excess fat.
2. Toss chicken with flour in a plastic bag, shaking off any excess.
3. Stir together the paprika, curry powder, cayenne pepper, ginger, sugar, tomato paste, chicken stock and lemon juice in the bowl of the slow cooker.
4. Turn chicken thighs in this mixture to coat evenly with the sauce.
5. Rinse chickpeas and drain well. Scatter over the chicken and stir gently to nestle the chickpeas between the chicken pieces and throughout the sauce.
6. Cover with lid and cook according to the times and settings specified.
7. Serve the chicken, topping each serving with a spoonful of yoghurt. Sprinkle torn mint leaves on top.

CROCKPOT	**low for 7–8 hours, high for 3½–4 hours**
SLOW COOKER	**low for 6–7 hours, high for 3–3½ hours**
SPEEDY SLOW COOKER	**low for 4½–5 hours high for 2¾–3 hours**

Tasty chicken wraps

Little morsels of chicken cooked in this lightly curried sauce make a succulent and tasty filling for wraps. This can also be served with rice or potatoes.

- 6 boneless, skinless chicken thighs (about 1 kg)
- 3 Tbsp flour
- 2 tsp curry powder
- 1 tsp smoked paprika
- 2 Tbsp apricot jam
- 2 Tbsp soy sauce
- 2 Tbsp tomato sauce (ketchup)
- ⅛ tsp cayenne pepper
- ¼ cup chicken stock

for the wraps

- 8 tortillas or other flat bread
- finely diced red onion
- chopped salad greens
- chopped tomatoes
- grated cheese
- Greek yoghurt or sour cream

SERVES 4–6

1. Trim chicken of excess fat, and cut into 2 cm pieces. Toss with flour in a plastic bag. Shake off any excess.
2. Place curry powder, paprika, apricot jam, soy sauce, tomato sauce, cayenne pepper and chicken stock in the slow cooker. Stir to combine.
3. Add chicken and stir gently so that all the chicken is coated with the sauce.
4. Cover with lid and cook according to the times and settings specified.
5. Warm the tortillas and place some of the chicken mixture in the centre of each one. Top with diced onion, chopped salad greens, chopped tomatoes and grated cheese. Fold in three sides of the tortilla to enclose the filling.
6. Serve immediately with a dollop of yoghurt or sour cream.

CROCKPOT	**low for 5–6 hours, high for 3–3½ hours**
SLOW COOKER	**low for 4½–5½ hours, high for 2½–3 hours**
SPEEDY SLOW COOKER	**low for 2¾–3 hours high for 2–2¼ hours**

Venison sausage and lentil ragoût (see p. 105)

Sausages

To rid sausages of excess fat I have always pre-browned them in a frying pan before putting them in the slow cooker. Nowadays I read the labels on the sausages and choose those containing low amounts of fat, so that the initial browning stage can be skipped. The amount of fat varies enormously from brand to brand. The lowest fat content I have seen is 7.5 per cent and the highest is 24.5 per cent.

I can buy a good selection of sausages containing different meats and flavourings, all containing less than 12 per cent fat, from my local supermarket.

If you choose low-fat sausages, you can put them straight into the slow cooker without any fear of an overly fatty sauce or of feeding your family an unnecessary amount of fat.

Hot and sour sausages

This is unpretentious, very tasty family fare. I am always surprised at just how popular it is.

1. Leave the sausages whole or twist then cut in half at the twist to form shorter sausages, and place in the slow cooker.
2. In a small bowl, mix together flour and brown sugar. Add soy sauce and mix until smooth. Add to the slow cooker.
3. Place crushed pineapple and juice, garlic, peanut butter, lime juice, chilli and chicken stock in the slow cooker and stir.
4. Cover with lid and cook according to the times and settings specified.
5. Thirty minutes prior to the end of the cooking, turn the slow cooker to high (if cooking on low) and stir in the capsicum and green peas.
6. Cover with lid and cook for the final half hour.
7. Serve with rice or creamy mashed potatoes and a green vegetable.

500 g sausages
1 Tbsp flour
1 Tbsp brown sugar
2 Tbsp soy sauce
1 x 225 g can crushed pineapple in juice
2 cloves garlic, crushed
3 Tbsp peanut butter, warmed
3 Tbsp lime juice
½ tsp prepared, chopped chilli
1¼ cups chicken stock
1 red capsicum, de-seeded and finely sliced
1 cup green peas, thawed if frozen

SERVES 4

CROCKPOT	**low for 6–7 hours, high for 3½–4 hours**
SLOW COOKER	**low for 5–6 hours, high for 3–3½ hours**
SPEEDY SLOW COOKER	**low for 4–5 hours, high for 2¼–2¾ hours**

Speedy sausage and bean casserole

A quick and delicious recipe for those hectic days. Other tinned beans, butter beans or cannellini beans can be used in place of red kidney beans — or you can use dried beans which you have cooked in the slow cooker (see p. 51).

- 8 or 9 sausages (about 700 g)
- 3 cloves garlic, crushed
- 1 x 400 g can diced tomatoes in juice
- ¼ cup tomato paste
- 1 Tbsp Worcestershire sauce
- 1 tsp sugar
- 1¼ cups beef stock
- 1 tsp dry mustard
- 1 x 400 g can red kidney beans, rinsed and drained, or 1½ cups cooked dried beans
- 2 Tbsp chopped fresh herbs

SERVES 4–6

1. Leave the sausages whole or twist then cut in half at the twist to form shorter sausages, and place in the slow cooker.
2. Add all the remaining ingredients except the fresh herbs to the slow cooker and stir gently to mix.
3. Cover with lid and cook according to the times and settings specified.
4. Garnish with fresh herbs.
5. Serve with a crusty bread or mashed potatoes and a green salad.

CROCKPOT	**low for 6½–7 hours, high for 3½–4 hours**
SLOW COOKER	**low for 6–7 hours, high for 3–3½ hours**
SPEEDY SLOW COOKER	**low for 4½–5½ hours, high for 2½–3 hours**

Spiced sausages with apple

The sharpness of the apple contrasts beautifully with the spicy sweetness of the sauce making this a popular family dish.

1. Leave sausages whole or twist then cut in half at the twist to form shorter sausages.
2. Place kumara in the slow cooker.
3. Add the sausages to the slow cooker, placing them evenly over the kumara.
4. Layer diced apple over the sausages.
5. In a medium bowl, mix together brown sugar, flour, mustard and ginger.
6. Add tomato sauce, Worcestershire sauce and balsamic vinegar and mix to a smooth paste.
7. Add apple juice to this mixture and stir.
8. Spoon over the apples and sausages. Cover with lid and cook according to the times and settings specified.
9. Sprinkle with chopped fresh parsley.
10. Serve with mashed potatoes or over rice with a green vegetable or a salad.

8 or 9 thick pork sausages (about 800 g)
350g kumara, peeled and diced into 2 cm cubes
2 medium, crisp eating apples (300 g) peeled, cored and diced
1 Tbsp brown sugar
2 Tbsp flour
1 tsp dry mustard
1 tsp ground ginger
3 Tbsp tomato sauce (ketchup)
2 Tbsp Worcestershire sauce
2 Tbsp balsamic vinegar
1½ cups apple juice
chopped parsley to garnish

SERVES 4–6

CROCKPOT	**low for 7½ –8½ hours, high for 4-4½ hours**
SLOW COOKER	**low for 7–8 hours, high for 3½–4 hours**
SPEEDY SLOW COOKER	**low for 4½–5 hours, high for 3–3½ hours**

Venison sausage and lentil ragoût

You can of course use any sausages for this but do choose brown lentils as they retain their shape when cooked. Their colour softens to a slightly paler shade than the kumara which is visually appealing.

During the long slow braise the lentils absorb the other flavours making this a really delicious meal in a pot. A tossed salad is the only accompaniment needed, although a crusty bread to mop up the juices goes well.

1. Leave sausages whole or twist then cut in half at twist to form shorter sausages. Place in slow cooker.
2. Add lentils, onion, lemon, garlic, ginger, tomato paste, chilli, kumara, chicken stock and rosemary to the slow cooker and stir.
3. Cover with lid and cook according to the times and settings specified.
4. Taste and season with salt and pepper.
5. Serve garnished with fresh rosemary and lemon slices.

CROCKPOT	high for 5–6 hours
SLOW COOKER	high for 4½–5 hours
SPEEDY SLOW COOKER	high for 3½–4 hours

- 7–8 venison sausages (500–600 g)
- 1 cup brown lentils, washed and drained
- 1 onion, finely chopped
- 1 lemon cut into eighths
- 3 cloves garlic, crushed
- 1½ Tbsp minced ginger
- 3 Tbsp tomato paste
- ½–1 tsp prepared, chopped chilli
- 500 g golden kumara, peeled and diced into 2 cm cubes
- 3½ cups chicken stock
- 2 Tbsp chopped fresh rosemary
- salt and pepper
- fresh rosemary and lemon slices to garnish

SERVES 4–6

Pork and Bacon Terrine (see p. 120)

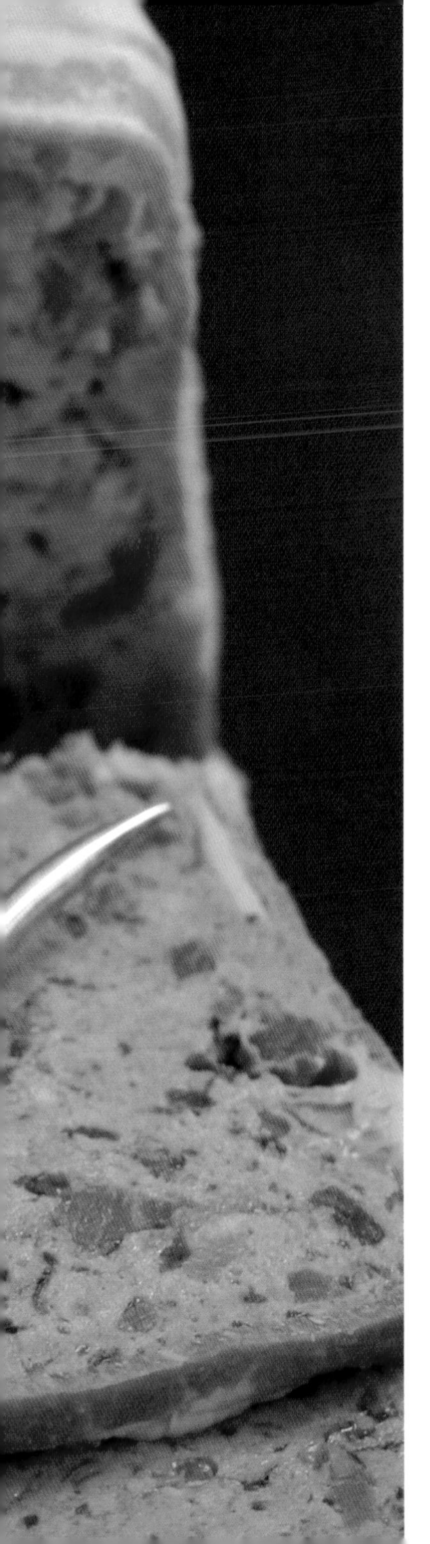

Mince

Because mince is finely ground it cooks quickly. If it is pre-browned in a frying pan it will stand prolonged cooking in the slow cooker without disintegrating into fine particles. However, without pre-browning it cooks in 3–4 hours on low in the slow cooker and the texture is good. It is still acceptable after 4–5 hours of cooking on low but I find the texture is unacceptable if cooking continues for a longer time.

I have given two recipes here for meat sauces which go straight into the slow cooker but they are not for all-day cooking. They will be at their best in approximately 3–3½ hours on low. However, meatballs in a sauce will be fine for 8 hours or more.

Mexican beef and beans

Everyone can serve themselves, spooning this mildly spiced beef and bean sauce onto a flour or corn tortilla. Pile on some extras such as finely chopped onions, tomatoes, shredded cheese, baby spinach leaves, coleslaw, yoghurt or sour cream. Fold in three sides of the tortilla to enclose the filling and it's ready to eat.

- 600 g quality beef mince
- 1 tsp prepared, chopped chilli
- 2 cloves garlic, crushed
- 3 Tbsp tomato paste
- 1 Tbsp flour
- 1 tsp dried oreganum
- ½ tsp ground cumin
- 1 x 400 g can diced tomatoes in juice
- 1 x 400 g can red kidney beans
- 1 x 400 g can whole kernel corn or 1½ cups frozen corn, thawed
- 1 red capsicum, de-seeded and finely sliced

SERVES 4–6

1. Crumble the beef in your fingers as you place it in the slow cooker, or break it up with a fork once inside the slow cooker.
2. Add the remaining ingredients and mix them all together with a fork, breaking up any remaining lumps of mince.
3. Cover with lid and cook according to the times and settings specified.
4. Serve wrapped in warm tortillas as suggested above or with rice.

CROCKPOT	**low for 4–4½ hours, high for 2-2½ hours**
SLOW COOKER	**low for 3–3½ hours, high for 1¾–2¼ hours**
SPEEDY SLOW COOKER	**low for 2 –2½ hours, high for 1½–2 hours**

Picadillo

Another quick and easy Mexican meat sauce for busy days. Children like this tasty mixture as long as it is not too spicy hot. Serve as a main dish with rice or in warm tortillas topped with some or all of the following: avocado slices, chopped lettuce, finely diced red onion, chopped tomatoes, and grated cheese.

- 600 g quality beef mince
- 2 cloves garlic, crushed
- 1x 32 g pkt onion soup mix
- 1 Tbsp flour
- ⅛ tsp cayenne pepper
- ½ tsp ground cumin
- 1 Tbsp vinegar
- 1 x 400 g can diced tomatoes in juice
- ¼ cup raisins
- 1 dessert apple, peeled, cored and finely chopped

SERVES 4–6

1. Crumble the meat in your fingers as you place it in the slow cooker, or break it up with a fork once inside the slow cooker.
2. Add the remaining ingredients and mix them all together with a fork, breaking up any remaining lumps of mince.
3. Cover with lid and cook according to the times and settings specified.
4. Serve in tortillas or with rice.

CROCKPOT	low for 4–4½ hours, high for 2–2½ hours
SLOW COOKER	low for 3–3½ hours, high for 1¾–2¼ hours
SPEEDY SLOW COOKER	low for 2 –2½ hours, high for 1½–2 hours

Spaghetti bolognese

Many and varied are the recipes for this famous Italian meat sauce. This slow cooker version is rich and tasty and benefits from a long, slow simmer.

1. Preheat slow cooker for 20 minutes
2. Heat 1 Tbsp oil in a frying pan to medium heat and add onion, garlic and bacon. Sauté until the onions are softened.
3. Spoon into the slow cooker.
4. Add more oil to the frying pan if necessary, increase the heat and stir in the mince. Stir frequently until the mince is no longer pink. Pour off any fat.
5. Reduce the heat to medium, sprinkle the flour over the mince and stir to combine. Add beef stock, tomatoes, red wine, tomato paste, marjoram, thyme and nutmeg and bring to the boil. Simmer for a minute or two.
6. Spoon into the slow cooker and stir. Cover with lid and cook according to the times and settings specified. Taste the sauce, adding salt and pepper if required.
7. Serve meat sauce over spaghetti. Top with grated Parmesan or other cheese.

1–2 Tbsp oil
1 large onion, finely chopped
2 cloves garlic, crushed
3 rashers lean bacon, trimmed and diced
1 kg quality beef mince
4 Tbsp flour
1 cup beef stock
1 x 400 g can diced tomatoes in juice
½ cup red wine
⅓ cup tomato paste
2 tsp dried marjoram
2 tsp dried thyme
½ tsp grated nutmeg
salt and pepper
Parmesan cheese to serve

SERVES 6–7

CROCKPOT	**low for 7–8 hours, high for 3–4 hours**
SLOW COOKER	**low for 6–6½ hours, high for 3–3½ hours**
SPEEDY SLOW COOKER	**low for 4¼–5 hours, high for 2½–3 hours**

Meatballs with mint

These little meatballs are subtly flavoured with mint. The slightly sweet, sour sauce complements this well.

1. In a bowl, combine mince, breadcrumbs, mint, lemon juice, soy sauce and egg.
2. Mix gently until well blended. With wet hands, form the mixture into balls about the size of golf balls (makes approximately 32).
3. Place the flour in a shallow bowl. Drop 4 of the meatballs in the bowl and rotate the bowl until the meatballs are well coated. Place the coated meatballs in the bottom of the slow cooker. Repeat with the remaining meatballs then place in the slow cooker with a second layer on top if necessary.
4. Combine beef stock, brown sugar, wine vinegar, soy sauce and red wine in a small bowl and stir to mix.
5. Drizzle this sauce over the meatballs in the slow cooker, trying to coat each one with some of the sauce.
6. Cover with lid and cook according to the times and settings specified.
7. Garnish with sprigs of mint and serve over rice or couscous.

700 g lean lamb or beef mince
¾ cup fresh breadcrumbs
2 Tbsp chopped fresh mint
1 Tbsp lemon juice
1 Tbsp soy sauce
1 egg, beaten
2 Tbsp flour

For the sauce
¾ cup beef stock
1 Tbsp brown sugar
2 Tbsp red wine vinegar
1 Tbsp soy sauce
¼ cup red wine
mint sprigs to garnish

SERVES 4–6

CROCKPOT	**low for 6–7 hours, high for 3–4 hours**
SLOW COOKER	**low for 5–6 hours, high for 2½–3¼ hours**
SPEEDY SLOW COOKER	**low for 4½–5½ hours, high for 2–2¼ hours**

Meatballs in tomato and red wine sauce

These aromatic meatballs, flavoured with cheese and cooked in a rich tomato sauce, are a favourite with everyone.

1. In a bowl combine the mince, breadcrumbs, cheese, cayenne pepper, parsley, soy sauce and egg.
2. Mix gently until well blended. With wet hands form the mixture into balls about the size of golf balls. Makes approximately 32 meatballs.
3. Place the flour in a shallow bowl. Drop 4 of the meatballs in the bowl and rotate the bowl until the meatballs are well coated. Place the coated meatballs in the bottom of the slow cooker. Repeat with the remaining meatballs, then place in the slow cooker with a second layer on top if necessary.
4. Combine sauce ingredients except the parsley in a small bowl and stir to mix.
5. Drizzle the sauce over the meatballs in the slow cooker, trying to coat each one with some of the sauce.
6. Cover with lid and cook according to the times and settings specified.
7. Garnish with parsley, and serve with noodles or potatoes and vegetables.

700 g quality beef or lamb mince
¾ cup soft breadcrumbs
3 Tbsp grated Parmesan or other cheese
¼ tsp cayenne pepper
2 Tbsp chopped fresh parsley
2 Tbsp soy sauce
1 egg, beaten
2–3 Tbsp flour

For the sauce

¼ cup finely chopped sundried tomatoes in oil, well drained (30 g)
1 cup beef stock
2 Tbsp tomato paste
½ cup red wine
2 tsp brown sugar
1½ tsp dried basil
chopped parsley to garnish

SERVES 4–6

CROCKPOT	**low for 6–7 hours, high for 3–4 hours**
SLOW COOKER	**low for 5–6 hours, high for 2½–3¼ hours**
SPEEDY SLOW COOKER	**low for 4½–5 hours, high for 2–2¼ hours**

Pork balls in honey soy sauce

These little meatballs are tender and succulent, easy to make and popular with both children and adults.

1. In a bowl combine pork mince, parsley, breadcrumbs, mustard and tomato paste.
2. Mix gently until well blended. With wet hands form the mixture into balls about the size of golf balls. Makes approximately 28 balls.
3. Place the flour in a shallow bowl. Drop 4 of the pork balls into the bowl and rotate the bowl until the pork balls are well coated. Place the coated meatballs in the bottom of the slow cooker. Repeat with the remaining meatballs, then place in the slow cooker with a second layer on top if necessary.
4. Combine sauce ingredients in a small bowl and stir to mix.
5. Drizzle the sauce over the pork balls in the slow cooker, trying to coat each one with some of the sauce.
6. Cover with lid and cook according to the times and settings specified.
7. Serve over rice or noodles, accompanied by broccoli or another green vegetable.

600 g pork mince
¼ cup chopped flat leaf parsley
½ cup soft breadcrumbs
1 Tbsp whole seed mustard
1 Tbsp tomato paste
2 Tbsp flour

Sauce

2 Tbsp honey
2 Tbsp soy sauce
2 tsp minced ginger
2 cloves garlic, crushed
1 Tbsp tomato paste
¾ tsp Chinese five spice
¾ cup chicken stock

SERVES 4–6

CROCKPOT	**low for 6–7 hours, high for 3–4 hours**
SLOW COOKER	**low for 5–6 hours, high for 2½–3 hours**
SPEEDY SLOW COOKER	**low for 4–4¼ hours, high for 2–2¼ hours**

Satay pork balls

These light and lovely pork balls flavoured with chilli and peanut are cooked in a mildly spiced coconut sauce.

700 g pork mince
1 cup soft breadcrumbs
3 Tbsp peanut butter, warmed
2 Tbsp soy sauce
2 Tbsp sweet chilli sauce

For the sauce
3 Tbsp peanut butter, warmed
1 Tbsp minced ginger
½–¾ tsp prepared chilli
1 Tbsp soy sauce
¾ cup light coconut milk
chopped chives to garnish

SERVES 4–6

1. In a bowl combine pork mince, breadcrumbs, peanut butter, soy sauce and sweet chilli sauce.
2. Mix gently until well blended. With wet hands, form the mixture into balls about the size of golf balls. Makes approximately 32 pork balls.
3. Place in the bottom of the slow cooker with a second layer on top if necessary.
4. Combine sauce ingredients in a medium-sized bowl and stir to mix.
5. Drizzle the sauce over the pork balls in the slow cooker, trying to coat each one with some of the sauce.
6. Cover with lid and cook according to the times and settings specified.
7. Sprinkle with chives and serve with rice or naan bread and a salad.

CROCKPOT	low for 6–7 hours, high for 3–3½ hours
SLOW COOKER	low for 5½–6½ hours, high for 2¾–3¼ hours
SPEEDY SLOW COOKER	low for 4–4½ hours, high for 2–2½ hours

Meatloaf

Meatloaf is wonderful comfort food, but gone are the days when it was regarded as cheap and standard fare. It now has a rather chic image and can be served in different ways: hot, with creamy mashed potatoes and a crisp cooked green vegetable; or cold, sliced thinly and presented on a platter with a variety of mustards, a good bread and a salad. Meatloaf travels well so is ideal to serve cold at picnics. Layered between thick slices of crusty bread, leftovers make delicious sandwiches.

Meatloaf from the slow cooker will not be as brown as an oven-baked one. This does not bother me and I serve it as is, just lightly browned. However, to enhance the appearance of the meatloaf, you can:

- Brush with a little dark soy sauce, barbecue sauce or tomato paste, before cooking;
- Sprinkle a little grated cheese on top of the meatloaf about twenty minutes prior to the end of cooking;
- Sprinkle chopped fresh herbs over the cooked meatloaf.

Meatloaf with herbs

1. Lightly oil the base and sides of the slow cooker.
2. In a large bowl combine all the ingredients for the meatloaf and, using either a fork or your hands, mix thoroughly.
3. Shape the mixture to make an oval or round loaf which will fit into the slow cooker.
4. Place the meatloaf in the slow cooker.
5. Cover with lid and cook according to the times and settings specified.
6. To remove the meatloaf from the slow cooker, use two large serving spoons, one on either side, and lift out. This is not a crumbly meatloaf so it will lift out easily.
7. Serve hot or cold.

CROCKPOT	**low for 7–8 hours, high for 3½–4 hours**
SLOW COOKER	**low for 6½–7½ hours, high for 3–3½ hours**
SPEEDY SLOW COOKER	**low for 5–5½ hours, high for 2½–3 hours**

900 g quality beef mince
1¼ cups fresh breadcrumbs
3 Tbsp tomato paste
3 Tbsp red wine or beef stock
2 eggs (size 6)
1 Tbsp Dijon mustard
1½ tsp dried basil
½ cup chopped flat leaf parsley

SERVES 8

Saucy meatloaf

This is a variation on the preceding recipe. The easy-to-make, tasty tomato sauce is spooned over the meatloaf in the slow cooker just prior to cooking.

Follow the recipe for 'Meatloaf with Herbs' on p. 117. When you have placed the meatloaf in the slow cooker, spoon the tomato sauce over the top.

1. Combine tomato paste, garlic, Worcestershire sauce, brown sugar and flour in a small bowl and mix well.
2. Add beef stock and red wine and stir until smooth.
3. Spoon over the meatloaf in the slow cooker immediately prior to cooking.
4. Cover with lid and cook according to the times and settings specified.
5. To serve hot, cut into thick slices and spoon sauce over the meatloaf.

For tomato sauce

¼ cup tomato paste

2 cloves garlic, crushed

1 Tbsp Worcestershire sauce

2 tsp brown sugar

2 Tbsp plain flour

¼ cup beef stock

3 Tbsp red wine or water

SERVES 8

CROCKPOT	**low for 7–8 hours, high for 3½–4 hours**
SLOW COOKER	**low for 6½–7½ hours, high for 3–3½ hours**
SPEEDY SLOW COOKER	**low for 5–5½ hours, high for 2½–3 hours**

Glazed country meatoaf

This makes a tasty midweek dinner and slices beautifully.

1. Lightly oil the base and sides of the cooker.
2. In a large bowl, combine all the ingredients for the meatloaf and, using either a fork or your hands, mix thoroughly.
3. Shape the mixture to make an oval or round loaf that will fit into the cooker.
4. Using a band of folded baking paper placed under the meatloaf makes it much easier to lift the meatloaf out of the cooker once cooking is complete. Fold a long piece of baking paper (50–60 cm) in half lengthways and then in half again lengthways.
5. Place the baking paper strip in the cooker, making sure the ends hang over the edges of the cooker. Place the meatloaf on the baking strip in the cooker.
6. Combine the Dijon mustard, tomato sauce, soy sauce and brown sugar in a small bowl then brush the top of the loaf with the mixture.
7. Tuck the ends of the baking paper in so they are inside the cooker.
8. Cover and cook according to the times and settings specified.
9. Lift the loaf out using the baking paper strips.
10. Cut into thick slices and serve hot with pan juices spooned over and a salad of fresh greens.

800 g quality beef mince
400 g sausage meat
1 cup fresh breadcrumbs
1 small onion, finely chopped
½ small red capsicum, finely chopped
3 cloves garlic, crushed
¼ tsp cayenne pepper
2 tsp dried oreganum
1 tsp salt
1/3 cup tomato sauce(ketchup)
2 eggs, beaten

glaze

1 Tbsp each Dijon mustard and tomato sauce (ketchup)
1 tsp each dark soy sauce and brown sugar

SERVES 8

CROCKPOT	**low for 7–8 hours, high for 3½-4 hours**
SLOW COOKER	**low for 6½–7½ hours, high for 3–3½ hours**
SPEEDY SLOW COOKER	**low for 5–5½ hours, high for 2½–3 hours**

Pork and bacon terrine

I find terrines are quick to make and very versatile. Serve with French bread for a substantial snack when entertaining friends for drinks and nibbles. A tossed salad and a good crusty bread are the perfect accompaniments when serving the terrine for lunch or dinner. As this terrine travels well, it is ideal picnic fare and any leftovers make gourmet sandwiches. Chillies, sundried tomatoes and rosemary add to the intense flavour of this terrine and these vibrant, colourful ingredients liberally fleck each slice.

Bake the terrine a day or two before it is required, giving it time to mature.

- 6 slices streaky bacon, to line the loaf tin
- 900 g trim pork mince
- 120 g lean bacon, trimmed and finely chopped
- ⅓ cup fresh breadcrumbs
- 1 small onion, finely chopped
- 3 plump cloves garlic, crushed
- 2 Tbsp finely chopped fresh rosemary
- ¼ cup chopped flat leaf parsley
- 50 g sundried tomatoes in oil (well drained), chopped
- 1 egg (size 7), beaten

1. Preheat the slow cooker for 20 minutes.
2. Place trivet in slow cooker. (Three $2 coins work well.)
3. Lightly oil the base and sides of a 7–8 cup capacity loaf tin, cake tin or casserole dish which will fit inside the slow cooker.
4. Line the loaf tin with the streaky bacon, placing the bacon across the tin and allowing the ends to drape over the sides of the dish.
5. Combine the remaining ingredients except the fresh herbs or salad leaves and pack into the bacon-lined loaf tin. Fold the overhanging bacon slices over the top of the meat mixture.
6. Cover tightly with foil. Using a foil strap (see p. 11), lift the loaf tin into the slow cooker and place on the trivet.

7. Pour enough boiling water into the slow cooker to come halfway up the sides of the loaf tin. Cover with lid and cook according to the times and settings specified.
8. Test that the juices are clear by inserting a skewer.
9. Using the foil strap, lift the tin from the slow cooker and cool for about an hour. Pour the juices which surround the terrine into a small bowl. Cover and refrigerate until cold. This liquid sets and is delicious to eat cold or can be used as a stock.
10. Remove the terrine from the loaf tin, wrap in foil and refrigerate overnight.
11. Garnish with fresh herbs or salad leaves. Serve sliced with French bread, tomatoes lightly drizzled with olive oil and marinated olives.

CROCKPOT	**low for 7–8 hours, high for 3½-4 hours**
SLOW COOKER	**low for 7–8 hours, high for 3½–4 hours**
SPEEDY SLOW COOKER	**low for 6–7 hours, high for 3–3½ hours**

¼ cup sweet chilli sauce
2 Tbsp balsamic vinegar
fresh herbs or salad leaves to garnish

SERVES 8 AS A MAIN COURSE

Beef and venison

Pre-browning of beef and venison in a frying pan is not necessary for flavour. The only other reason to pre-brown is to eliminate excess fat. However, fat can be eliminated quickly and easily by trimming visible fat from the meat prior to cooking.

Beef curry with cashew nuts

This is a mild curry with a rich creamy sauce. Serve it with rice and a green vegetable or salad.

1 Cut steak into 2 cm cubes and place in the slow cooker.
2 Add onion, apple and carrot, and stir.
3 Combine flour, coriander, cumin, paprika, cayenne pepper and salt, and mix well.
4 Sprinkle this mixture over the meat and vegetables in the slow cooker and stir.
5 Pour coconut milk onto meat and vegetables, and stir thoroughly.
6 Cover with lid and cook according to the times and settings specified.
7 Sprinkle with cashew nuts and serve.

CROCKPOT	**low for 9–10 hours, high for 4½–5 hours**
SLOW COOKER	**low for 8–9 hours, high for 4–4½ hours**
SPEEDY SLOW COOKER	**low for 6–6½ hours, high for 3½–4 hours**

1 kg blade or chuck steak
1 onion, finely chopped
1 dessert apple, peeled, cored and sliced
1 medium carrot, peeled and diced finely
4 Tbsp flour
2 tsp ground coriander
1 tsp ground cumin
1 tsp paprika
¼ tsp cayenne pepper
½ tsp salt
¾ cup light coconut milk
½ cup roughly chopped cashew nuts

SERVES 4–5

Beef in beer

This is a distinctive and vigorous winter dish. The meat simmers in a dark, full-bodied ale which imparts its rich aroma, colour and flavour to the braise. Near the end of the cooking time, redcurrant jelly is added, giving a wonderful sheen to the sauce.

1. Combine the steak, onion and garlic in the slow cooker.
2. Sprinkle with flour and toss well.
3. Mix together tomato paste, salt, pepper and nutmeg. Add the beer and stir to combine. Pour this over the meat and onion and mix well.
4. Cover with lid and cook according to the times and settings specified.
5. Thirty minutes before the end of the cooking time, turn the control to high (if cooking on low).
6. Stir in cornflour mixed to a paste with the 3 Tbsp beer.
7. Add the redcurrant jelly and stir.
8. Cover with lid and cook for the remaining half hour. Serve with freshly cooked noodles and a salad.

1.2 kg blade, topside or chuck steak cut into 2.5 cm cubes
1 medium onion, finely chopped
2–3 cloves garlic, crushed
¼ cup flour
2 Tbsp tomato paste
salt and freshly ground black pepper
½ tsp ground nutmeg
1½ cups dark beer, stout or Guinness
3 Tbsp cornflour
3 Tbsp dark beer, stout or Guinness (second measure)
3 Tbsp redcurrant jelly

SERVES 6–7

CROCKPOT	low for 9–10 hours, high for 4½–5 hours
SLOW COOKER	low for 8–9 hours, high for 4–4½ hours
SPEEDY SLOW COOKER	low for 6½–7 hours, high for 3¾–4 hours

Beef in Burgundy

This classic, intensely flavoursome beef stew for which French cuisine is famous is so simple to make in a slow cooker.

1.3 kg blade steak, diced into 2–3 cm cubes
250 g lean bacon rashers, trimmed and chopped
1 small red onion, finely chopped
3 cloves garlic, crushed
¼ cup flour
1¾ cups red wine
2 Tbsp tomato paste
2 tsp dried thyme
2 Tbsp redcurrant jelly
1½ Tbsp finely chopped fresh rosemary
300 g Portabello mushrooms, wiped and sliced
salt
chopped fresh thyme to garnish

1. Combine steak, bacon, onion and garlic in the slow cooker. Sprinkle the flour over the top and stir.
2. Mix red wine and tomato paste together and pour over the meat in the slow cooker. Scatter the thyme over the top and stir.
3. Cover with lid and cook according to the times and settings specified.
4. Half an hour prior to serving, add redcurrant jelly, rosemary and mushrooms, and stir gently to combine.
5. Turn the control to high (if cooking on low), cover with lid and continue cooking for the final 30 minutes.
6. Check seasoning, and add salt if necessary.
7. Scatter chopped fresh thyme on top and serve.

CROCKPOT	**low for 9–10 hours, high for 4½–5 hours**
SLOW COOKER	**low for 8–9 hours, high for 4–4½ hours**
SPEEDY SLOW COOKER	**low for 6½–7 hours, high for 3¾–4 hours**

SERVES 6–7

Beef rollups

Thin slices of beef are rolled around a tasty mushroom and bacon stuffing, and cooked in a deliciously rich mushroom sauce.

1. Combine bacon, mushrooms, breadcrumbs, egg, basil and red wine or beef stock and mix lightly until just combined.
2. Divide the stuffing mixture evenly between each piece of steak and roll up.
3. Place beef rolls in the slow cooker.
4. Combine the soup mix and red wine to form a smooth paste. Add beef stock and stir, then spoon over the rolls in the slow cooker.
5. Cover with lid and cook according to the times and settings specified.
6. Half an hour before completion of cooking, turn the control to high (if cooking on low). Add sliced mushrooms, gently pushing the mushrooms down into the sauce.
7. Cover with lid and continue to cook for the final 30 minutes.
8. Garnish with fresh herbs. Serve on rice or pasta, or with mashed potatoes and a green vegetable.

CROCKPOT	**low for 8–9 hours, high for 4–4½ hours**
SLOW COOKER	**low for 7–8 hours, high for 3½–4 hours**
SPEEDY SLOW COOKER	**low for 5–6 hours, high for 3–3½ hours**

6–8 pieces beef schnitzel (600–700 g)

for the stuffing

120 g lean bacon, trimmed and finely chopped
140 g Portabello mushrooms, wiped and finely chopped
1 cup soft breadcrumbs
1 egg, beaten
1 tsp dried basil
3 Tbsp red wine or beef stock

for the sauce

1 x 32 g pkt French onion (or mushroom or onion) soup mix
¼ cup red wine
½ cup beef stock
200 g Portabello mushrooms, wiped and sliced
fresh herbs to garnish

SERVES 5

Braised beef and vegetables with cheese and chive dumplings

This is a wonderfully aromatic dish in which the rich flavours of the beef and red wine are complemented by the gentle sweetness of kumara and leeks.

1.1 kg blade steak, diced into 2 cm cubes
¼ cup flour
300 g kumara, peeled and diced into 2cm cubes
250 g cleaned, trimmed and sliced leeks, (½ cm slices)
3 cloves garlic, crushed
1 x 400 g can diced tomatoes in juice
1½ tsp each onion salt and dried thyme
1 Tbsp Dijon mustard
1 cup red wine
salt

SERVES 6

1. Toss the steak cubes in flour. Set aside.
2. Place the kumara, leeks and garlic in the slow cooker and stir.
3. Add the meat.
4. Combine the tomatoes, onion salt, thyme, mustard and wine and pour over the meat. Stir a little to ensure the liquid flows around all the ingredients, taking care to keep the vegetables submerged.
5. Cover with lid and cook according to the times and settings.
6. Forty minutes before the completion of the cooking, turn the control to high (if cooking on low). Taste and add salt if necessary.
7. Prepare the Cheese and Chive Dumplings (see page 130) and add to the slow cooker approximately 30 minutes before completion of cooking.

CROCKPOT	low for 9–10 hours, high for 5–5½ hours
SLOW COOKER	low for 8–9 hours, high for 4½–5½ hours
SPEEDY SLOW COOKER	low for 6½–7 hours, high for 4½–5 hours

Cheese and chive dumplings

These light and tender dumplings make a delicious topping for many casseroles and soups.

1. In a medium-sized bowl, stir the cheese into the flour and toss to mix.
2. Combine milk, vinegar, butter, egg and chives and stir into the flour to make a soft dough.
3. Form into 8 dumplings and place on the top of the bubbling stew.
4. Cover with lid and cook for about 30 minutes, until the dumplings are puffed and firm to the touch. The dumplings will not brown and this does not bother me. But, if you like, place the ceramic liner under a medium to hot grill for 6–7 minutes to brown before serving.
5. Serve immediately. Spoon the casserole onto heated plates, topping each serving with a dumpling or two.

70 g grated tasty cheese
200 g self-raising flour
100 ml milk
1 tsp white vinegar
30 g butter, melted
1 egg, size 6, beaten
3 Tbsp chopped chives

SERVES 6

CROCKPOT	**high for approx 30 minutes**
SLOW COOKER	**high for approx 30 minutes**
SPEEDY SLOW COOKER	**high for 30 minutes**

Beef stroganoff

This dish is very simple but special enough for any occasion. The beef is cooked until tender in a tomato-based sauce with a hint of garlic. The Portabello mushrooms give a richness and depth to the sauce.

1 kg blade or chuck steak
¼ cup flour
freshly ground black pepper
1 small onion, finely chopped
3 cloves garlic, crushed
1 x 400 g can chopped tomatoes in juice
3 Tbsp tomato paste
1 tsp beef stock powder
2 Tbsp dry sherry
200 g Portabello mushrooms, sliced
1 cup light and creamy evaporated milk
3 Tbsp chopped fresh parsley

SERVES 4–5

1. Cut the beef into thin strips, dredge in the flour seasoned with pepper and place in the slow cooker.
2. Add onion, garlic, tomatoes, tomato paste, beef stock powder and sherry. Stir well to combine all the ingredients thoroughly.
3. Cover with lid and cook according to the times and settings specified.
4. Thirty minutes prior to serving, turn the control to high (if cooking on low), and add the mushrooms. Cover with lid and continue cooking.
5. Ten minutes before serving stir in the evaporated milk. Cover with lid and complete the cooking.
6. Sprinkle with parsley. Serve with creamy mashed potatoes or buttered noodles and a green salad.

CROCKPOT	**low for 8–10 hours, high for 4–5 hours**
SLOW COOKER	**low for 7–8 hours, high for 3½–4 hours**
SPEEDY SLOW COOKER	**low for 5–6 hours, high for 3–3½ hours**

Braised oxtail with raisins and pine nuts

Everywhere beef is farmed, oxtail will be available. The older the animal, the larger the tail — and the chunkier, meatier joints have the best flavour. The small skinny joints are best in the soup pot.

Oxtail comes rather high in fat but with careful trimming this fat is almost eliminated. I prefer to cook this braise a day ahead, chill overnight and remove any excess fat from the surface — then reheat and serve.

As it cooks, the braise develops wonderfully complex flavours and deepens to a dark mahogany colour.

3 meaty oxtails, jointed (about 1.8 kg, once the small tail end pieces have been removed)
½ cup flour
olive oil spray
1 large onion, finely chopped
4 cloves garlic, crushed
1½ Tbsp dark brown sugar
1½ Tbsp minced ginger
2 Tbsp soy sauce
2 Tbsp balsamic vinegar

1. Preheat the slow cooker for 20 minutes.
2. Trim off excess fat and roll pieces of oxtail in the flour. Heat a large frying pan to medium–high heat. Spray with oil, add the oxtail a few pieces at a time and brown well. Continue to spray with oil when necessary to prevent the meat sticking to the pan.
3. Transfer the browned joints to the slow cooker.
4. Reduce the frying pan heat to moderate, and spray with oil.
5. Sprinkle any remaining flour over the onion, add the onion and garlic to the pan and sauté for about 5 minutes until golden.

6. Add the brown sugar, ginger, soy sauce, balsamic vinegar, beef stock and red wine. Stir well and bring to the boil. Pour the contents of the frying pan into the slow cooker. Cover with lid and cook according to the times and settings specified.
7. Once the cooking is complete, if serving immediately, press folded paper towels over the surface to absorb any fat. Stir in the raisins and pine nuts and serve.
8. If cooking ahead of time, refrigerate overnight and next day scoop off any fat which has risen to the surface. Reheat and stir in the raisins and pine nuts just prior to serving.

CROCKPOT	**high for 5–6 hours**
SLOW COOKER	**high for 4¾–5¼ hours**
SPEEDY SLOW COOKER	**high for 4¼–4¾ hours**

1 tsp dried beef stock

1 cup red wine

⅓ cup raisins

3 Tbsp pine nuts

SERVES 4–5

Braised venison with blueberries

Venison is now widely available at supermarkets and farmers' markets. All but the most tender of roasts and steaks should be braised or casseroled. Meat from the shoulder, neck and breast is ideal for long, slow cooking.

The flavour of venison is enriched by sharp, sweet and spicy ingredients. These all mingle together, deepening to a superbly rich braise.

1 kg venison, diced into 2–3 cm cubes
4 Tbsp plain flour
3 large cloves garlic, crushed
zest of one lemon
zest of one orange
¾ cup orange juice
2 Tbsp tomato paste
1 Tbsp minced ginger
1 tsp prepared, chopped chilli
¾ cup red wine
180 g Portabello mushrooms, wiped and sliced
180 g blueberries, thawed if frozen
salt to taste
fresh thyme to garnish

SERVES 5–6

1. Pat the meat dry with paper towels.
2. Place the venison in the slow cooker. Add the flour and toss to mix.
3. Add the garlic, lemon and orange zest, orange juice, tomato paste, ginger, chilli and red wine. Stir gently to ensure all ingredients are well combined.
4. Cover with lid and cook according to the times and settings specified.
5. Forty minutes before the cooking time is complete, turn the control to high (if cooking on low). Add the mushrooms and blueberries and stir gently to ensure all the ingredients are well combined.
6. Cover with lid and complete the cooking. Taste, and add salt if necessary. Sprinkle fresh thyme leaves on top, and serve with creamy mashed potatoes and a green vegetable or salad.

CROCKPOT	**low for 8–10 hours, high for 4–5 hours**
SLOW COOKER	**low for 7–8 hours, high for 3½–4 hours**
SPEEDY SLOW COOKER	**low for 5½–6 hours, high for 3–3¼ hours**

Chilli con carne

This wonderful savoury mix of chilli, meat and beans which originated in Texas works particularly well in the slow cooker.

1. Combine meat, onions and garlic in the slow cooker and sprinkle with flour, cayenne pepper, paprika, cumin and salt. Toss together.
2. In a small bowl, mix tomatoes, tomato paste and wine and pour over the meat and onions in the slow cooker and stir to combine.
3. Cover with lid and cook according to the times and settings specified.
4. Forty-five minutes before the end of the cooking time, turn the control to high (if cooking on low) and add the beans.
5. Cover with lid and continue cooking for the final three-quarters of an hour until the beans are heated through.

CROCKPOT	**low for 9–11 hours, high for 4–5 hours**
SLOW COOKER	**low for 8–9 hours, high for 3¾–4¼ hours**
SPEEDY SLOW COOKER	**low for 6–7 hours, high for 3¼–3½ hours**

1.1 kg chuck or blade steak, diced into 2–3 cm cubes
1 medium onion, finely chopped
2 cloves garlic, crushed
4 Tbsp flour
½ tsp cayenne pepper
2 tsp paprika
1 tsp ground cumin
½ tsp salt
1 x 400 g can diced tomatoes in juice
⅓ cup tomato paste
⅓ cup red wine
2 x 310 g cans red kidney beans, rinsed and well drained

SERVES 6

Corned beef

Here are several options for cooking this cut, which has been the mainstay for many families over the years. Jazz up the cooking liquid so that the corned beef, when it emerges meltingly tender, will have absorbed some of the flavours from the cooking liquid.

Heat the liquid in a kettle or microwave until hot then pour it over the corned beef in the preheated slow cooker. If the liquid is cold it will take too long for cooking to begin.

I cook the vegetables to accompany the corned beef separately.

If the corned beef is not cooked to tender perfection in the time given it is probably due to the way the beef has been cured. I suggest buying corned beef from a trusted family butcher.

Traditional corned beef

1.5 kg corned beef, brisket, silverside or pickled pork
2 onions, peeled, halved and studded with 10 whole cloves
1 Tbsp black peppercorns
3 Tbsp wine vinegar
3 Tbsp raw sugar
hot water

SERVES 6–7

1. Preheat the slow cooker for 20 minutes.
2. Rinse the meat in cold water and pat dry.
3. Place the meat in the slow cooker with onions, black peppercorns, vinegar and raw sugar and enough hot water to barely cover the meat.
4. Cover with lid and cook according to the times and settings specified.
5. Once cooked, carve into thin slices and serve with creamy mashed potatoes, lightly sautéed cabbage, or other vegetables of your choice, and either Chilli Remoulade or Horseradish Cream (see p. 140).

CROCKPOT	low for 8–10 hours, high for 4–5 hours
SLOW COOKER	low for 7–8 hours, high for 3–4 hours
SPEEDY SLOW COOKER	low for 5½–6 hours, high for 3–3¼ hours

Corned beef gingered up

1.5 kg corned beef, brisket, silverside or pickled pork
1 x 1.5 litre bottle dry ginger ale, heated in saucepan or microwave
1 Tbsp ground ginger
1 Tbsp honey
hot water

SERVES 6–7

1. Preheat the slow cooker for 20 minutes.
2. Rinse the meat in cold water and pat dry.
3. Place the meat in the slow cooker and add ginger ale, ground ginger, honey and enough hot water to barely cover the meat.
4. Cover with lid and cook according to the times and settings specified.
5. Once the corned beef is cooked, carve into thin slices and serve with creamy mashed potatoes, lightly sautéed cabbage, or other vegetables of your choice, and either Chilli Remoulade or Horseradish Cream (see p. 140).

CROCKPOT	low for 8–10 hours, high for 4–5 hours
SLOW COOKER	low for 7–8 hours, high for 3–4 hours
SPEEDY SLOW COOKER	low for 5½–6 hours, high for 3–3¼ hours

Spiced corned beef

1. Preheat the slow cooker for 20 minutes.
2. Rinse the meat in cold water and pat dry.
3. Place the meat in the slow cooker and add pickling spices, golden syrup, wine vinegar and enough hot water to barely cover the meat.
4. Cover with lid and cook according to the times and settings specified.
5. Once the corned beef is cooked, carve into thin slices and serve with creamy mashed potatoes, lightly sautéed cabbage, or other vegetables of your choice, and either Chilli Remoulade or Horseradish Cream (see p. 140).

1.5 kg corned beef, brisket, silverside or pickled pork
½–¾ of a 25 g packet whole pickling spices
2 Tbsp golden syrup
2 Tbsp wine vinegar
hot water

SERVES 6–7

CROCKPOT	**low for 8–10 hours, high for 4–5 hours**
SLOW COOKER	**low for 7–8 hours, high for 3–4 hours**
SPEEDY SLOW COOKER	**low for 5½–6 hours, high for 3–3¼ hours**

Corned beef with ale and orange

1. Preheat the slow cooker for 20 minutes.
2. Rinse the meat in cold water and pat dry.
3. Place the meat in the slow cooker with light ale, maple syrup, orange zest, orange juice and enough hot water to barely cover the meat.
4. Cover with lid and cook according to the times and settings specified.
5. Once the corned beef is cooked, carve into thin slices and serve with creamy mashed potatoes, lightly sautéed cabbage, or other vegetables of your choice, and either Chilli Remoulade or Horseradish Cream (see p. 140).

CROCKPOT	low for 8–10 hours, high for 4–5 hours
SLOW COOKER	low for 7–8 hours, high for 3–4 hours
SPEEDY SLOW COOKER	low for 5½–6 hours, high for 3–3¼ hours

1.5 kg corned beef, brisket, silverside or pickled pork
1 x 350 ml bottle light ale
3 Tbsp maple syrup
grated zest of one orange
1 cup orange juice
hot water

SERVES 6–7

Sauces for corned beef

Chilli remoulade

This French mayonnaise-based cold sauce is usually served with meat or fish. It is also sometimes flavoured with anchovies. If desired, add 2–3 finely chopped anchovies to the mayonnaise along with the other ingredients and stir through.

½ cup mayonnaise
½ cup low fat sour cream
1 Tbsp wholegrain mustard
½ tsp prepared, chopped chilli
2 Tbsp finely chopped spring onions or chives
1 Tbsp finely chopped parsley
1 Tbsp chopped capers
2 Tbsp lemon juice

1. Combine all the ingredients.
2. Mix well and chill.

Horseradish cream

150 ml low fat sour cream
4 tsp commercially prepared horseradish sauce
½ tsp sugar
2 tsp Dijon mustard
1 Tbsp white wine vinegar

1. Combine all the ingredients.
2. Spoon into a serving dish and chill.

Oriental beef pot roast

All these wonderful flavours have time to meld and the gentle heat keeps the meat moist and tender.

1. Trim meat of excess fat.
2. Place soy sauce, chilli, sherry or rice wine, ginger, sugar and Chinese five spice in the slow cooker and mix well. Add beef and turn, so that the mixture coats all surfaces of the meat.
3. Cover with lid and cook according to the times and settings specified.
4. Thirty minutes prior to serving, turn control to high (if cooking on low). Combine cornflour and sherry and mix to a smooth paste. Stir into the juices in the slow cooker.
5. Replace lid and continue cooking for the final half hour.
6. Remove meat from the slow cooker. Slice and arrange on a platter, spooning some of the gravy over the meat. Serve remaining gravy separately.

1.5 kg beef pot roast (bolar, trout or topside)
2 Tbsp soy sauce
½–1 tsp prepared, minced chilli
3 Tbsp sherry or rice wine
1 tsp ground ginger
2 Tbsp brown sugar
1 tsp Chinese five spice
2 Tbsp cornflour
2 Tbsp sherry (second measure)

SERVES 6–8

CROCKPOT	**low for 9–11 hours, high for 4½–5 hours**
SLOW COOKER	**low for 7½–8½ hours, high for 3¾–4¼ hours**
SPEEDY SLOW COOKER	**low for 5½–6 hours, high for 3–3½ hours**

Country beef casserole

A long-standing family favourite, this is a complete meal in a pot.

1. Trim any fat from the meat. Cut meat into 2 cm cubes.
2. Arrange onion, potatoes and carrots on the base of the slow cooker.
3. Toss the meat in the flour and place on top of the vegetables. Add the bay leaves, thyme and onion salt.
4. Combine the mustard, soy sauce and beef stock in a small bowl and stir. Pour over the meat in the slow cooker.
5. Cover with lid and cook according to the times and settings specified.
6. Twenty minutes before completion of cooking, turn the control to high (if cooking on low). Add the green peas and stir.
7. Cover and cook for the remaining twenty minutes.
8. Sprinkle with thyme and serve.

CROCKPOT	**low for 9–10 hours, high for 4½–5 hours**
SLOW COOKER	**low for 8–9 hours, high for 4–5 hours**
SPEEDY SLOW COOKER	**low for 7–8 hours, high for 4–5 hours**

1 kg chuck or blade steak
1 small onion, finely chopped
3 large potatoes (700 g), peeled and diced into 2 cm cubes
2 medium carrots (200 g), peeled and finely diced
3 Tbsp flour
2 bay leaves
1 tsp dried thyme
½ tsp onion salt
1½ Tbsp Dijon mustard
2 Tbsp soy sauce
1¼ cups beef stock
250 g frozen green peas, thawed
fresh thyme leaves to garnish

SERVES 5

Beef pot roast with apricots and prunes

This is one of my favourite recipes, as it is especially easy but always looks impressive.

Cooking the beef pot roast in an oven bag inside the slow cooker ensures the meat emerges succulent and extremely tender. If preferred, the beef can be placed directly into the slow cooker and it will still be delicious.

1.5 kg beef pot roast (bolar, trout or topside)
1 Tbsp honey
1 Tbsp soy sauce
½ tsp ground cinnamon
1 Tbsp redcurrant jelly
100 g Central Otago dried apricots, halved
100 g pitted prunes
50 g raisins
fresh fennel to garnish

1. Trim excess fat from meat.
2. Mix together honey, soy sauce and cinnamon. Brush the mixture over the beef, using a pastry brush.
3. Place the meat in an oven bag. Seal and perforate the bag and place in the slow cooker, with perforated side at the top to allow steam to escape.
4. Cover with lid and cook according to the times and settings specified.
5. Forty minutes before completion of cooking, split open and remove the oven bag, leaving the meat and juices in the slow cooker.
6. Turn the control to high (if cooking on low), and add the redcurrant jelly and dried fruits. Push them down into the liquid.
7. Cover with lid and continue to cook for the remaining 40 minutes.
8. Serve meat sliced, with juices and fruit spooned over, garnished with fennel.

9 Alternatively, serve with gravy. To make gravy, pour cooking juices into a small saucepan. Stir in cornflour mixed to a paste with wine or water and bring to the boil, continuing to stir until gravy thickens. Pour thickened gravy into a gravy boat to serve.

for gravy

beef topside cooking juices

2 Tbsp cornflour

2 Tbsp wine (white or red) or water

SERVES 6

CROCKPOT	**low for 8–10 hours, high for 4–5 hours**
SLOW COOKER	**low for 7–8 hours, high for 3½–4 hours**
SPEEDY SLOW COOKER	**low for 3½–3¾ hours, high for 3–3¼ hours**

Ox tongue

1 ox tongue (1–1½ kg)

1 medium onion, sliced

2 bay leaves

1 Tbsp cider vinegar

6 whole cloves

boiling water

for jellied tongue

1 Tbsp gelatin

½ cup cold cooking liquid

1½ cups boiling cooking liquid

SERVES 6

1. Preheat slow cooker for 20 minutes.
2. Place the washed tongue in the slow cooker and add the remaining ingredients, with enough boiling water to completely cover the tongue.
3. Cover with lid and cook according to the times and settings specified. Save the cooking liquid if jellying the tongue.
4. When cooked, cut out the undesirable portions of the root end, including any small bones. Remove the skin by slitting from the root end to the tip on the underside. Loosen the skin at the root and peel towards the tip.
5. To make Jellied Tongue, press cooked tongue tightly into a mould. (A round cake tin works well.) Add gelatin to cold cooking liquid and stir. When soft, add boiling cooking liquid and stir until completely dissolved. Pour carefully into the mould to cover the tongue and chill. Turn out onto a flat serving dish.

CROCKPOT	**low for 10–12 hours, high for 5–6 hours**
SLOW COOKER	**low for 9–10 hours, high for 4¾–5½ hours**
SPEEDY SLOW COOKER	**low for 8–9 hours, high for 4½–5 hours**

Spiced beef stew

Simple beef stews like this one lend themselves to long, slow simmering. If possible, plan ahead and leave the meat to marinate overnight in the spicy sauce. I like to serve this with creamy mashed potatoes and a crisp green vegetable, such as broccoli or green beans.

1 Cut meat into 2 cm cubes and set aside.
2 Combine flour, brown sugar, curry powder, ginger, mixed spice and salt in the slow cooker.
3 Add Worcestershire sauce and vinegar and mix to a smooth paste. Then add tomato sauce, sherry and water and stir. Place meat in the slow cooker and stir again.
4 If time permits, cover with lid and stand in a cool place for 2 hours or overnight in the refrigerator.
5 Cover with lid and cook according to the times and settings specified.
6 Serve with potatoes and a green vegetable.

CROCKPOT	**low for 8–10 hours, high for 4–5 hours**
SLOW COOKER	**low for 7–8 hours, high for 3½–4 hours**
SPEEDY SLOW COOKER	**low for 5½–6 hours, high for 3–3½ hours**

1 kg chuck or blade steak
3 Tbsp flour
2 Tbsp brown sugar
1 tsp curry powder
½ tsp ground ginger
½ tsp mixed spice
½ tsp salt
1 Tbsp Worcestershire sauce
2 Tbsp vinegar
3 Tbsp tomato sauce
2 Tbsp sherry
3 Tbsp water

SERVES 4–5

Stifado

A great favourite, this aromatic Greek stew is an amalgam of sweet and sour tastes which give the dish its unique flavour. Goat or sheep's milk feta holds its shape well when added to the stew, whereas cows' milk feta disintegrates slightly.

1 Toss cubed steak with flour in the slow cooker.

2 Add cumin, garlic, brown sugar, salt, tomato paste, red wine vinegar, beef stock and red wine, and stir to combine.

3 Add clove-studded onion, cinnamon sticks and bay leaves, pushing them down so they are covered by the liquid.

4 Cover with lid and cook according to the times and settings specified.

5 Thirty minutes before the cooking time is complete, stir in the currants.

6 Cover with lid and continue to cook for the final half hour.

7 Remove bay leaves, cinnamon sticks and clove-studded onion.

8 Very gently stir in the feta and serve.

9 Serve with a salad and garlic mashed potatoes, couscous or crusty bread to mop up the juices.

CROCKPOT	low for 8–9 hours, high for 4–4½ hours
SLOW COOKER	low for 7–8 hours, high for 3½–4 hours
SPEEDY SLOW COOKER	low for 5¾–6 hours, high for 3½–4 hours

1.2 kg blade or chuck steak, diced into 2 cm pieces
4 Tbsp flour
1 tsp ground cumin
3 cloves garlic, crushed
1 Tbsp brown sugar
1 tsp salt
¼ cup tomato paste
¼ cup red wine vinegar
½ cup beef stock
1 cup red wine
1 small onion, peeled and studded with 10 whole cloves
2 cinnamon sticks
3 bay leaves
½ cup currants
150 g feta, cut into small cubes

SERVES 6–7

Swiss steak

This wonderfully rich, tomato-flavoured braise was fashionable during the early 1960s but has subsequently disappeared from most cooks' repertoires. Warm, comforting braises and casseroles are enjoying a revival, and this one is perfect for the slow cooker.

1 kg chuck or blade steak, cut into small serving-sized pieces
¼ cup flour
freshly ground black pepper
1 medium onion, finely chopped
2 medium carrots, peeled and finely diced
¾ cup tomato purée
½ cup good beef stock
½ cup red wine

SERVES 6

1. Combine the steak, flour and black pepper in a plastic bag and shake well, until the flour evenly coats the meat. Remove meat and set aside.
2. Add onion and carrots to the remaining flour in the plastic bag and shake thoroughly. Place the onion and carrots in the slow cooker and shake any flour remaining in the bag over the top.
3. Place the pieces of meat on top of the vegetables.
4. Mix together tomato purée, beef stock and red wine, and pour over the meat and vegetables.
5. Very gently push the meat and vegetables around a little so that the liquid flows throughout.
6. Cover with lid and cook according to the times and settings specified.
7. Serve with green vegetables or a salad.

CROCKPOT	**low for 8–10 hours, high for 4–5 hours**
SLOW COOKER	**low for 7–8 hours, high for 3½–4 hours**
SPEEDY SLOW COOKER	**low for 5½–6 hours, high for 3¼–3½ hours**

Venison ragoût

Prime venison steak cooks in a few minutes on a very hot pan or grill. However, the slow cooker comes into its own for the tougher cuts, cooking them to a succulent tenderness.

Juniper berries give a spicy background flavour, and blackcurrant juice and port emphasise the gaminess of the venison as they meld together to form this superbly rich sauce.

1. Place venison and onion in the slow cooker.
2. Combine nutmeg, flour and thyme and sprinkle over the meat. Toss to mix.
3. Pour blackcurrant juice and port over the meat. Add juniper berries and chopped rosemary. Stir the juice and port thoroughly through the meat cubes.
4. Cover with lid and cook according to the times and settings specified.
5. Ten minutes before serving, stir in the light evaporated milk. Cover with lid and complete the cooking process. Check seasoning, and add salt if necessary.
6. Garnish with rosemary, and serve with glazed root vegetables and creamy mashed potatoes.

CROCKPOT	**low for 8–10 hours, high for 4–5 hours**
SLOW COOKER	**low for 7–8 hours, high for 3½–4 hours**
SPEEDY SLOW COOKER	**low for 5½–6 hours, high for 3–3½ hours**

1.1 kg venison, diced into 2–3 cm cubes
1 onion, finely chopped
¼ tsp ground nutmeg
¼ cup flour
2 tsp dried thyme
½ cup blackcurrant juice, unsweetened
½ cup port
5 juniper berries, crushed
1 Tbsp chopped fresh rosemary
½ cup light and creamy evaporated milk
salt
sprigs of rosemary to garnish

SERVES 4–5

Lamb Shanks with Red Wine and Rosemary (see p. 158)

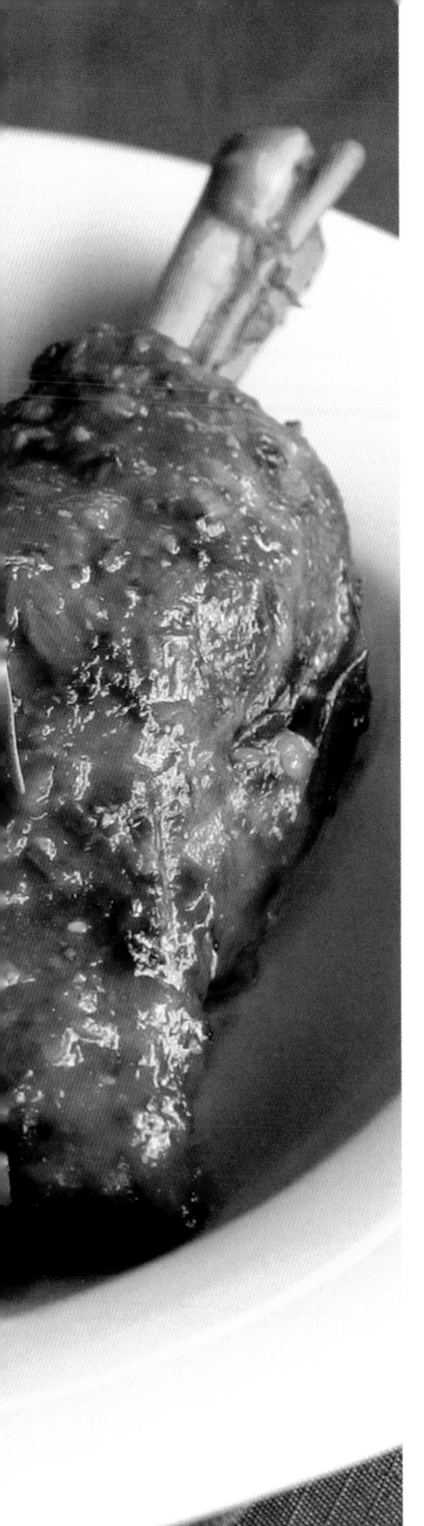

Lamb

Pre-browning of lamb in a frying pan is not necessary for flavour. The only other reason to pre-brown is to eliminate excess fat. However, fat can be eliminated quickly and easily by trimming visible fat from the meat prior to cooking.

Curried lamb chops

Lightly curried chops make an ideal family meal which is quick to assemble.

Choose lean lamb, hogget or mutton chops and trim well to remove excess fat. If using mutton, increase the cooking time by one hour on low or half an hour on high.

One kilogram of cubed lamb, hogget or mutton may be substituted for the chops.

- 6 lamb leg or shoulder chops
- 1–2 Tbsp mild curry powder
- 4 Tbsp flour
- 1 onion, finely chopped
- ½ cup chicken stock
- 1 large dessert apple, peeled, cored and sliced
- 2 Tbsp lemon juice
- ¼ cup sultanas

SERVES 6

1. Trim the chops of excess fat.
2. Combine curry powder and flour and sprinkle over the chops. Set aside.
3. Spread the chopped onion evenly over the base of the slow cooker and arrange the chops on top.
4. Pour the chicken stock over the chops.
5. Toss the apple slices in the lemon juice and place them on top of the chops.
6. Sprinkle with sultanas.
7. Cover with lid and cook according to the times and settings specified.
8. Serve over rice.

CROCKPOT	**low for 7–8 hours, high for 3½–4 hours**
SLOW COOKER	**low for 6–7 hours, high for 3–3½ hours**
SPEEDY SLOW COOKER	**low for 4½–5 hours, high for 2¾–3 hours**

Tomato topped lamb chops

Choose lean lamb, hogget or mutton chops for this recipe and trim off excess fat. The cooking times I have given above are for lamb — increase by half an hour for hogget, and one hour for mutton.

1. Trim chops of excess fat.
2. Combine brown sugar, ginger, nutmeg, tomato paste, wine vinegar and wine or vegetable stock in a small bowl and mix well.
3. Add tomatoes and stir to combine.
4. Place a layer of chops on the base of the slow cooker and spoon over some of the spicy tomato mixture.
5. Place another layer of chops on top and spoon some of the sauce over them.
6. Continue until all the chops are layered in the slow cooker. Spoon remaining sauce over the top.
7. Cover with lid and cook according to the times and settings specified.
8. Thirty minutes before cooking time is complete, turn the control to high (if cooking on low). Mix the cornflour to a paste with the water or wine and stir into the juices in the slow cooker.
9. Cover with lid and cook for the remaining half hour.
10. Serve hot sprinkled with mint.

6–8 lamb leg or shoulder chops (1 kg–1.4 kg)
3 Tbsp brown sugar
¾ tsp ground ginger
½ tsp ground nutmeg
4 Tbsp tomato paste
3 Tbsp wine vinegar
2 Tbsp red wine or vegetable stock
1 x 400 g can diced tomatoes in juice
2 Tbsp cornflour
2 Tbsp water or red wine
chopped fresh mint to garnish

SERVES 6

CROCKPOT	**low for 7–8 hours, high for 3½–4 hours**
SLOW COOKER	**low for 6–7 hours, high for 3–3½ hours**
SPEEDY SLOW COOKER	**low for 4½–5 hours, high for 2¾–3 hours**

Honeyed lamb with orange and thyme

Herbs, spices and honey make a wonderful coating for a juicy succulent lamb.

1. Trim lamb of any visible fat.
2. Place the orange slices on the base of the slow cooker.
3. Mix together honey, mustard, ginger, nutmeg, balsamic vinegar and thyme. Brush the mixture over the lamb using a pastry brush, covering all surfaces.
4. Place lamb on the orange slices, cover with lid and cook according to the times and settings specified.
5. Remove the lamb from the slow cooker and pour the accumulated juices from the slow cooker into a small saucepan. Return meat to the slow cooker to keep warm while you make the gravy.
6. In a small bowl mix cornflour and orange juice to a smooth paste.
7. Bring the juices in the saucepan to the boil. Remove saucepan from heat and stir in the cornflour paste.
8. Replace the saucepan on the heat and stirring constantly bring to the boil, reduce heat and simmer for a couple of minutes.
9. Slice the meat and arrange on a platter. Garnish with sprigs of thyme. Spoon some of the gravy over the top, and serve remaining gravy separately.

CROCKPOT	**low for 8–10 hours, high for 4–5 hours**
SLOW COOKER	**low for 7–8 hours, high for 3½–4 hours**
SPEEDY SLOW COOKER	**low for 4–5 hours, high for 3–3¼ hours**

½ leg lamb, approx. 1.5 kg
2 oranges, each sliced into 5 slices
2 Tbsp honey, warmed
2 Tbsp Dijon mustard
3 tsp ground ginger
½ tsp ground nutmeg
1 Tbsp balsamic vinegar
1 Tbsp chopped fresh thyme leaves
thyme sprigs to garnish

for the gravy

1 Tbsp cornflour
2 Tbsp orange juice

SERVES 5–6

Lamb shanks with red wine and rosemary

Lamb shanks make excellent eating but need slow simmering in an aromatic liquid to emerge succulent and tender.

Because of their irregular shape, being much wider at one end than the other, shanks are not easy to brown in a frying pan. I skip this step when cooking them in the slow cooker. I prefer to cook the shanks the day before, as this allows me to skim off any fat once the dish is cold. Alternatively, once the cooking is complete, lift the shanks from the slow cooker and place a double thickness of paper towel on top of the sauce to blot up any fat. Replace shanks and serve.

Lamb shanks are usually sold with the leg bone cut in half. When preparing them for the slow cooker, continue the cut and slice into two pieces.

Both shanks and knuckles are from the lower leg. The bigger and meatier shank is from the hind leg while the knuckle is from the fore leg.

6 lamb shanks, halved, or
  6 lamb knuckles
1 small onion, finely chopped
2 cloves garlic, crushed
¼ cup flour
2½ tsp ground coriander

1. Trim any excess fat from the shanks.
2. Place onion and garlic in the slow cooker.
3. Toss shanks in flour. Sprinkle any remaining flour over onions and garlic in the slow cooker and place shanks on top.

4 Combine the remaining ingredients in a small bowl and stir until thoroughly mixed. Spoon this mixture over the lamb shanks.

5 Cover with lid and cook according to the times and settings specified.

6 Serve with mashed potatoes and a green vegetable or salad.

CROCKPOT	**low for 9–11 hours, high for 4½–5 hours**
SLOW COOKER	**low for 8–9 hours, high for 4–4½ hours**
SPEEDY SLOW COOKER	**low for 6½–7 hours, high for 3¾–4 hours**

¼ cup beef stock

¾ cup red wine

2 Tbsp tomato paste

grated zest and juice of 1 orange

2 Tbsp chopped fresh rosemary

SERVES 6–8

Lamb with peanut sauce

A pot roast of lamb in an Indonesian-style sauce is a surprising combination but one that works well. Hogget or mutton may be substituted for the lamb but extend the cooking times: an extra half hour for hogget, and one hour for mutton.

1 thick end leg of lamb
2 cloves garlic, crushed
2 Tbsp brown sugar
1 tsp ground coriander
2 Tbsp soy sauce
½ tsp prepared, chopped chilli
grated zest of one lemon
4 Tbsp lemon juice
⅓ cup crunchy peanut butter
1 Tbsp cornflour
1 Tbsp lemon juice (second measure)

SERVES 4–5

1. Trim meat of excess fat and place meat in slow cooker.
2. Combine garlic, brown sugar, coriander, soy sauce, chilli, lemon zest and juice and mix well.
3. With a pastry brush, generously paint all surfaces of the lamb with this mixture. Drizzle any that remains over the top of the lamb.
4. Cover with lid and cook according to the times and settings specified.
5. Thirty minutes prior to completion of cooking, turn the control to high (if cooking on low). Stir in the peanut butter. Mix the cornflour and lemon juice to a smooth paste and stir into the juices in the cooker.
6. Cover with lid and cook for the remaining half hour.
7. Remove lamb from the slow cooker. Slice and arrange on a platter. Spoon some of the sauce over the top, and serve remaining sauce separately.

CROCKPOT	**low for 8–9½ hours, high for 4–4½ hours**
SLOW COOKER	**low for 7–8 hours, high for 3½–4 hours**
SPEEDY SLOW COOKER	**low for 4–5 hours, high for 3–3¼ hours**

Lamb with tamarillos

Sliced tamarillos add a special piquancy to this lamb casserole.

To skin tamarillos, plunge them into boiling water for two minutes and then peel.

1. Toss lamb with flour in a plastic bag. Shake off any excess.
2. Place lamb in the slow cooker and add onion, garlic, ginger, chicken stock, lemon juice, soy sauce and honey.
3. Cover with lid and cook according to the times and settings specified.
4. About half an hour before serving, add sliced tamarillos to the slow cooker. Cover with lid and continue to cook for the final 30 minutes.
5. Sprinkle chopped fresh thyme or parsley on top.

1 kg lean lamb, cubed
4 Tbsp flour
1 small onion, finely chopped
2 cloves garlic, crushed
1 Tbsp minced ginger
1 cup chicken stock
2 Tbsp lemon juice
2 Tbsp soy sauce
2 Tbsp honey
4 tamarillos, peeled and sliced
fresh thyme or parsley to garnish

SERVES 4

CROCKPOT	**low for 8–9 hours, high for 4–4½ hours**
SLOW COOKER	**low for 7–8 hours, high for 3½–4 hours**
SPEEDY SLOW COOKER	**low for 5–5½ hours, high for 3¼–3½ hours**

Leg of lamb with mint and pecan stuffing

A fragrant mixture of rosemary, balsamic vinegar and mustard coats the lamb but does not overpower it. The stuffing of fresh mint, lemon juice and pecans is delicious with lamb.

Most butchers are happy to bone a leg of lamb but it is a good idea to give them twenty-four hours' notice. If hogget is used in place of lamb, increase the cooking time by one hour on low or half an hour on high.

1 Trim any excess fat from the leg.

2 To make the stuffing: in a bowl place breadcrumbs, mint, onion, pecans, salt, pepper, butter and lemon juice and mix together lightly until just combined, adding a little more lemon juice if necessary.

3 Place the stuffing in the leg cavity and fold the meat around it, using string to tie it into a neat parcel.

4 Combine balsamic vinegar, mustard and rosemary. Brush this mixture over all surfaces of the lamb, using a pastry brush.

5 Place lamb in the slow cooker, cover with lid and cook according to the times and settings specified.

1 boned leg of lamb or hogget, approx. 1.8 kg (a 2.2 kg leg weighs approx. 1.8 kg once boned)
1¼ cups day-old breadcrumbs
3 Tbsp chopped fresh mint
½ small onion, finely chopped
½ cup roughly chopped pecans
salt and freshly ground black pepper
2 Tbsp melted butter
2 Tbsp lemon juice (approx.)

6. Remove meat from the slow cooker. Pour all the juices in the slow cooker into a small saucepan. Return the meat to the slow cooker, replace the lid and keep it warm while you make the gravy.
7. Mix the cornflour to a smooth paste with the red wine, and stir into the juices in the saucepan.
8. Stirring constantly, bring to the boil. Reduce heat and simmer for 2–3 minutes.
9. Slice the lamb, arrange on a platter and ladle some of the gravy over the top. Serve remaining gravy separately.

1½ Tbsp balsamic vinegar

2 Tbsp Dijon mustard

¼ cup chopped fresh rosemary

3 Tbsp cornflour

3 Tbsp red wine

SERVES 7–8

CROCKPOT	**low for 8–10 hours, high for 4–5 hours**
SLOW COOKER	**low for 7–8 hours, high for 3½–4 hours**
SPEEDY SLOW COOKER	**low for 5¾–6¼ hours, high for 3¼–3½ hours**

Simple lamb pot roast

The preparation is minimal, but the long, slow cooking ensures the meat is tender and juicy. Mutton can be cooked like this too — simply increase the cooking time by an hour. A beef rolled roast or piece of chuck, blade, bolar or topside can also be cooked this way.

forequarter lamb or hogget
1x 32 g pkt onion soup mix
1 Tbsp brown sugar
1 tsp paprika
¼ cup red wine, chicken stock or vegetable stock

SERVES 4–6

1. Ask your butcher to joint the forequarter so that it will fit into the slow cooker. The forequarter can be boned if preferred.
2. Remove excess fat and place meat in the slow cooker.
3. Combine the soup mix, brown sugar and paprika, and mix well. Pat this mixture onto the top of the meat.
4. Place the meat in the slow cooker and sprinkle any remaining topping over the meat.
5. Pour the red wine or stock around the meat.
6. Cover with lid and cook according to the times and settings specified.
7. Serve meat sliced, with the juices from the slow cooker spooned over the top.

CROCKPOT	**low for 8–9 hours, high for 4–4½ hours**
SLOW COOKER	**low for 7–8 hours, high for 3½–4 hours**
SPEEDY SLOW COOKER	**low for 5¾–6¼ hours, high for 3¼–3½ hours**

Persian lamb tagine

Tagines are Middle Eastern stews which combine fruits and spices with meat. Lamb has a special affinity with apricots, and the ginger and cinnamon add a slightly spicy sweetness to this rich dish.

1.25 kg boneless lean lamb, cut into 2–3 cm cubes
1 medium onion, finely chopped
¼ cup flour
¾ tsp ground ginger
1 tsp ground cinnamon
2 tsp paprika
1¼ cups vegetable or chicken stock
150 g dried apricots
3 Tbsp lemon juice
½ cup pinenuts
salt to taste

SERVES 6

1. Place lamb and onion in the slow cooker and sprinkle flour, ginger, cinnamon and paprika over the top. Toss well.
2. Add stock and stir to combine.
3. Cover with lid and cook according to the times and settings specified.
4. Three-quarters of an hour before completion of cooking, turn the control to high (if cooking on low). Add the apricots, and push them down into the liquid in the slow cooker.
5. Replace lid and continue cooking.
6. Ten minutes prior to completion of cooking, add lemon juice and pinenuts. Stir well and check seasoning. Add salt if necessary. Cover with lid and cook for the final ten minutes.
7. Serve over couscous.

CROCKPOT	**low for 8–10 hours, high for 4–5 hours**
SLOW COOKER	**low for 7–8 hours, high for 3½–4 hours**
SPEEDY SLOW COOKER	**low for 5¾–6¼ hours, high for 3¼–3½ hours**

Pork in Coconut Lime Sauce (see p. 179)

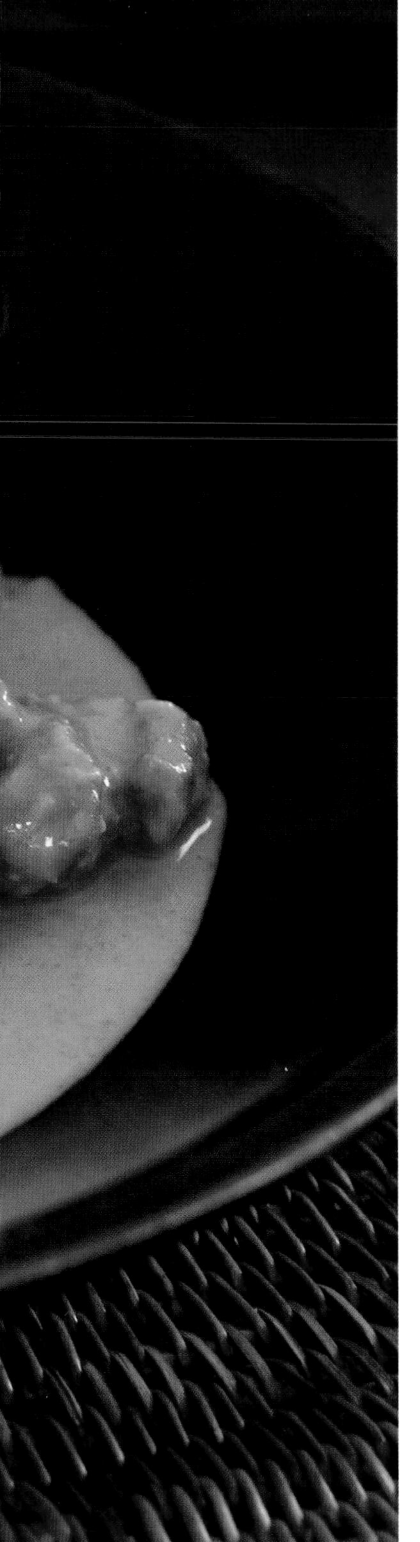

Pork

Pre-browning of pork in a frying pan is not necessary for flavour. The only other reason to pre-brown is to eliminate excess fat. However, fat can be eliminated quickly and easily by trimming visible fat from the meat prior to cooking.

Apple spiced pork

This is so simple. The pork is braised with apple juice and spices and the meat emerges succulent, tender and very flavoursome. Serve just as is, or with Blackcurrant Sauce (see p. 169).

Pork leg or shoulder roast is often on special at supermarkets and makes for economical eating.

1 pork leg or shoulder, 1.5–2 kg
2 Tbsp Dijon mustard
2 tsp ground ginger
½ tsp ground cinnamon
½ cup apple juice
fresh thyme to garnish

SERVES 6–8

1. Cut skin from pork, removing any fat with it.
2. Mix mustard, ground ginger and cinnamon together and brush this mixture over the pork, using a pastry brush.
3. Place pork in the slow cooker and pour apple juice around it.
4. Cover with lid and cook according to the times and settings specified.
5. Remove the pork from the slow cooker and slice onto a large serving platter.
6. Spoon the cooking juices over the pork and garnish with thyme, or serve with Blackcurrant Sauce (see p. 169).

CROCKPOT	**low for 8–10 hours, high for 4–5 hours**
SLOW COOKER	**low for 7–8 hours, high for 3½–4 hours**
SPEEDY SLOW COOKER	**low for 4–5 hours, high for 3–3½ hours**

Blackcurrant sauce

The wonderfully intense concentration of flavours in this easy-to-make sauce is magical with pork. A real treat which requires little effort.

2 medium dessert apples (350 g total)
20 g butter
¼ tsp ground cinnamon
300 g blackcurrants, thawed if frozen
1 tsp cornflour
¾ cup apple juice
3 Tbsp redcurrant jelly or blackcurrant jam

1. Peel, core and slice the apples.
2. Heat butter in a small frying pan, add apple slices and gently sauté for about 10 minutes until golden.
3. Add cinnamon and blackcurrants and their juice to the frying pan. Mix cornflour and apple juice together until smooth and add to the frying pan.
4. Gently bring to the boil, stirring, and simmer for 2–3 minutes.
5. Stir in jelly or jam until dissolved. Remove from the heat.
6. Spoon some of the Blackcurrant Sauce over the meat to serve. Pour remaining sauce into a deep bowl and serve with the meat.

Chilli peanut pork

A dish heady with wonderfully spicy flavours. The pork pieces cook until meltingly tender in this mild, aromatic sauce.

1. Turn the slow cooker to the setting you intend to cook on.
2. Place peanut butter in the slow cooker. As the slow cooker warms, the peanut butter will soften.
3. Toss diced pork with the flour in a plastic bag, shaking off any excess. Set aside.
4. Add garlic, ginger, cumin, coriander, sweet chilli sauce, lime or lemon juice, soy sauce and chicken stock to the slow cooker. Once the peanut butter has softened, stir to combine.
5. Add pork and stir again.
6. Cover with lid and cook according to the times and settings specified.
7. Slice spring onions finely on the diagonal and stir into the pork.
8. Serve over rice.

⅓ cup peanut butter
1 kg lean pork, diced into 2 cm cubes
4 Tbsp flour
2 cloves garlic, crushed
1 Tbsp minced ginger
1 tsp ground cumin
1 tsp ground coriander
4 Tbsp sweet chilli sauce
3 Tbsp lime or lemon juice
2 Tbsp soy sauce
1 cup chicken stock
2 spring onions

SERVES 4–6

CROCKPOT	**low for 8–9 hours, high for 4–4½ hours**
SLOW COOKER	**low for 7–8 hours, high for 3½–4 hours**
SPEEDY SLOW COOKER	**low for 5–5½ hours, high for 3–3¼ hours**

Citrus pork

This delicious way of cooking a piece of pork leg or shoulder is easy and quick to prepare. The pork, coated with spices, cooks to succulent tenderness in the slightly sweet, citrus sauce.

1 piece of pork leg or shoulder, 1.5–2 kg
1 Tbsp ground ginger
2 tsp paprika
½ tsp ground cinnamon
3 Tbsp marmalade
zest of 1 orange
4 Tbsp orange juice
3 Tbsp balsamic vinegar
2 Tbsp finely chopped rosemary
rosemary sprigs to garnish

for the gravy
2 Tbsp cornflour
3 Tbsp orange juice

SERVES 6–8

1. Cut the skin from the pork removing any fat with it.
2. Mix ginger, paprika and cinnamon together and rub well into the meat.
3. Place meat in an oven bag and place in the slow cooker.
4. Combine marmalade, orange zest, orange juice, balsamic vinegar and rosemary. Pour this around the pork in the oven bag and seal.
5. Snip a small hole in the top of the bag to allow excess steam to escape. Cover with lid and cook according to the times and settings specified.
6. Lift the pork in its bag from the slow cooker. Remove the bag and place the pork on a serving platter. Slice the pork and serve with the cooking juices spooned over the top. Garnish with rosemary sprigs.
7. Alternatively serve the pork with gravy. To make gravy: pour cooking juices into a small saucepan. Stir in cornflour mixed to a paste with orange juice and heat, stirring until gravy thickens. Simmer for 2–3 minutes. Serve alongside the pork.

CROCKPOT	low for 8–10 hours, high for 4–5 hours
SLOW COOKER	low for 7–8 hours, high for 3½–4 hours
SPEEDY SLOW COOKER	low for 4–5 hours, high for 3–3½ hours

Hawaiian pork

With its sharp, sweet and sour flavours, this uncomplicated pork and pineapple casserole is a great favourite.

1. Toss the pork with the flour in a plastic bag. Shake off any excess. Place pork in slow cooker.
2. In a small bowl combine sugar, ginger, paprika and chicken stock powder and stir. Add vinegar, soy sauce and reserved pineapple juice and mix well.
3. Pour over the pork in the slow cooker.
4. Add pineapple pieces and capsicum and stir gently.
5. Cover with lid and cook according to the times and settings specified.
6. Garnish with herbs and serve with rice.

CROCKPOT	**low for 8–9 hours, high for 4–4½ hours**
SLOW COOKER	**low for 7–8 hours, high for 3½–4 hours**
SPEEDY SLOW COOKER	**low for 5–5½ hours, high for 3–3¼ hours**

800 g lean pork, diced into 2 cm cubes
3 Tbsp flour
3 Tbsp brown sugar
1 tsp ground ginger
2 tsp paprika
½ tsp chicken stock powder
¼ cup wine vinegar
2 Tbsp soy sauce
1 x 440 g can pineapple pieces in juice, drained and juice reserved
1 large red capsicum, de-seeded and finely sliced
fresh herbs to garnish

SERVES 4–5

Pickled pork and maple syrup

Whenever I serve this dish the response is overwhelmingly enthusiastic. The pickled pork is gently poached in apple juice and maple syrup, both of which impart their distinctive flavours and aromas to the meat. Serve just as is, or with Winter Fruits Sauce (see p. 174). Alternatively, serve with Chilli Remoulade or Horseradish Cream (p. 140).

1.5 kg piece of pickled pork
¼ cup maple syrup
750 ml apple juice

SERVES 6–7

1. Preheat the slow cooker for 20 minutes.
2. Trim meat of any excess fat and place meat in the slow cooker. Add maple syrup to the slow cooker. Pour apple juice into a suitable container and heat in a microwave or saucepan until hot.
3. Pour hot apple juice over meat in the slow cooker and turn the meat over in the aromatic liquid.
4. Cover with lid and cook according to the times and settings specified. If convenient, turn the meat halfway through the cooking process.
5. Remove the meat from the slow cooker. Slice and arrange on a platter. Serve with Winter Fruits Sauce (see p. 174) if desired.

CROCKPOT	low for 8–10 hours, high for 4–5 hours
SLOW COOKER	low for 7–8 hours, high for 3½–4 hours
SPEEDY SLOW COOKER	low for 6–6½ hours, high for 3–3¼ hours

Winter fruits sauce

This sauce, perfect with hot or cold meats, complements pork well and is absolutely delicious for a special occasion.

½ cup red wine
¾ cup apple juice
2 Tbsp lemon juice
80 g dried figs chopped
80 g dates chopped
80 g pitted prunes chopped

1. Place red wine, apple juice, lemon juice and figs in a small saucepan.
2. Bring to the boil over a gentle heat. Cover, reduce heat to very low and simmer for about a minute. Stir in the dates and prunes and continue to simmer for 4–5 minutes until the fruit is soft but still holds its shape.
3. Tip into a serving bowl and chill until required.
4. Serve Winter Fruits Sauce at room temperature with hot or cold meats.

Pork chops with apple

The sweet, sharp flavours of the kumara and apple balance superbly the richness of the pork. I prefer to use golden kumara in this dish as it does not darken once peeled, and its vibrant colour adds great visual appeal.

- 6 lean pork chops
- ¼ cup flour
- 1 medium kumara (300 g), peeled and diced into 1–2 cm cubes
- 2 Tbsp balsamic vinegar
- 2 Tbsp soy sauce
- 1½ Tbsp minced ginger
- 2 medium dessert apples (360 g total), peeled, cored and sliced
- 2 Tbsp lemon juice
- 2 Tbsp maple syrup
- 1½ Tbsp finely chopped fresh rosemary

SERVES 6

1. Trim chops of excess fat.
2. Sprinkle flour over the chops, shaking off excess.
3. Place kumara in the slow cooker.
4. Sprinkle remaining flour over kumara. Stir and spread evenly over the base of the slow cooker, and arrange chops on top.
5. Combine balsamic vinegar, soy sauce and ginger, and spoon this mixture over the chops.
6. Toss apple slices in lemon juice and place on top of the meat.
7. Drizzle maple syrup over the apples and sprinkle with rosemary.
8. Cover with lid and cook according to the times and settings specified.

CROCKPOT	**low for 8–9 hours, high for 4–4½ hours**
SLOW COOKER	**low for 7–8 hours, high for 3½–4 hours**
SPEEDY SLOW COOKER	**low for 5½–6 hours, high for 2½–3 hours**

Pork cassoulet

There are many versions of this legendary French dish, all based on dried white beans cooked with a combination of meats. This simple adaptation is tasty, gutsy and perfect for a fireside supper.

600 g lean pork, diced into 3 cm cubes
3 Tbsp flour
1 onion, finely chopped
4–5 pork sausages (450 g)
2 cured chorizo sausages (120 g)
2 x 400 g cans Cannellini beans
1 x 400 g can diced tomatoes in juice
¼ cup tomato paste
¾ cup chicken stock
1½ tsp dried thyme
¾ tsp ground allspice
2 Tbsp chopped fresh thyme or parsley

1. Toss pork with flour in a plastic bag. Shake off any excess.
2. Spread onion evenly over base of the slow cooker.
3. Leave pork sausages whole or twist then cut in half at the twist to form shorter sausages. Place in slow cooker.
4. Slice chorizo on the diagonal, 1 cm wide, and add to the slow cooker.
5. Place floured pork pieces in the slow cooker.
6. Rinse and drain beans well. Add to the slow cooker.
7. In a bowl mix together diced tomatoes, tomato paste, chicken stock, thyme and allspice. Pour evenly over the contents of the slow cooker.
8. Cover with lid and cook according to the times and settings specified.
9. Sprinkle with fresh herbs and serve.

SERVES 6–7

CROCKPOT	**low for 9–9½ hours, high for 4–5 hours**
SLOW COOKER	**low for 8–9 hours, high for 4–4½ hours**
SPEEDY SLOW COOKER	**low for 6–7 hours, high for 3–3½ hours**

Pork hocks in Chinese barbecue Sauce

Pork hocks vary quite considerably in size and price, but can make an economical and tasty meal. If preferred, a piece of pork leg or shoulder roast may be substituted for the hocks.

1 or 2 meaty pork hocks which fit inside the cooker, or a piece of pork leg or shoulder roast 1.3–1.5 kg
3 Tbsp soy sauce.
3 Tbsp rice wine or sherry
3 cloves garlic, crushed
1 Tbsp minced ginger
½–1 tsp prepared, chopped chilli
1 tsp Chinese five spice
2 tsp brown sugar
chopped spring onions to garnish

SERVES 6–7

1. Remove skin from the pork.
2. Combine soy sauce, rice wine or sherry, garlic, ginger, chilli, Chinese five spice and sugar in the slow cooker and stir well to mix.
3. Place pork into the slow cooker and turn so that it is well coated with the sauce.
4. Cover with lid and cook following the times and settings specified.
5. Cut meat into generous slices and serve with Asian noodles. Spoon the sauce over the meat and garnish with spring onions.

CROCKPOT	**low for 8–9 hours, high for 4½–5 hours**
SLOW COOKER	**low for 7–8 hours, high for 3½–4 hours**
SPEEDY SLOW COOKER	**low for 5–5½ hours, high for 3–3½ hours**

Pork in coconut lime sauce

In this easily assembled dish the spicy taste of the curry paste and the sharp taste of lime beautifully offset the richness of the coconut cream and pork.

1. Toss diced pork with the flour in a plastic bag, and shake off any excess.
2. Place red curry paste, brown sugar, garlic, ginger, soy sauce, lime juice and coconut cream or milk in the slow cooker, and stir to combine.
3. Add pork and diced kumara and stir again, so that all the pieces of pork and kumara are coated with the sauce.
4. Cover with lid and cook according to the times and settings specified.
5. Thirty minutes prior to serving, turn the slow cooker to high (if cooking on low) and stir in the red capsicum.
6. Cover with lid and cook for the final half hour.
7. Serve over rice and garnish with chopped coriander or mint.

1 kg lean pork, diced into 2 cm cubes
4 Tbsp flour
3–4 tsp red curry paste
1 Tbsp brown sugar
3 cloves garlic, crushed
1 Tbsp minced ginger
1 Tbsp soy sauce
3 Tbsp lime juice
1⅓ cups light coconut cream or light coconut milk
450 g golden kumara, peeled and diced into 2 cm cubes
1 red capsicum, de-seeded and finely sliced
chopped coriander or mint to garnish

SERVES 4–6

CROCKPOT	**low for 8½–9½ hours, high for 4½–5 hours**
SLOW COOKER	**low for 8–9 hours, high for 4–4½ hours**
SPEEDY SLOW COOKER	**low for 6–6½ hours, high for 3¼–3½ hours**

Apricot and Citrus Cheesecakes (see p. 186)

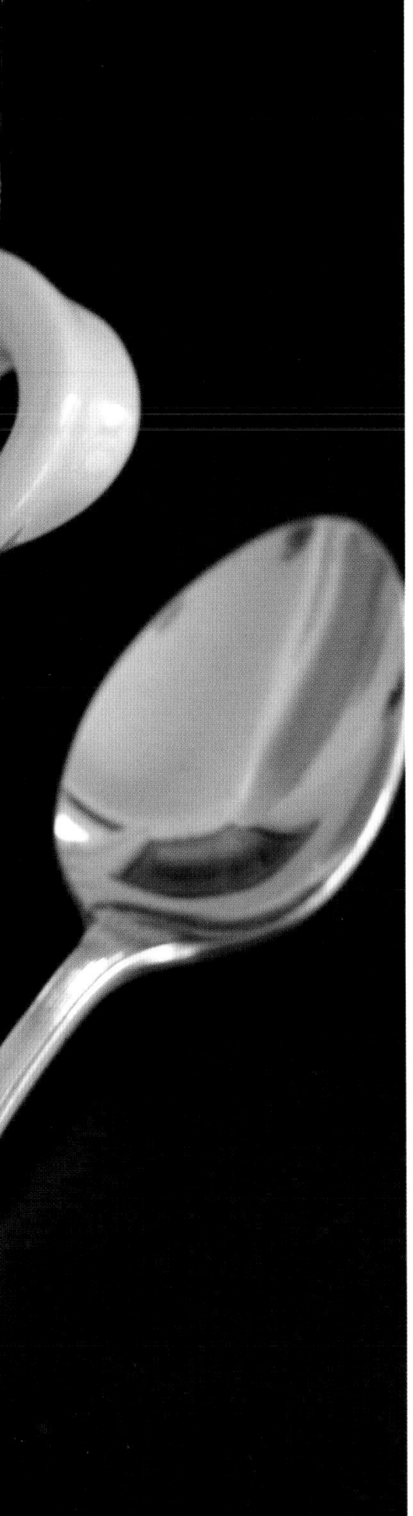

Puddings

When cooking dinner for family or friends, I have often wished I had a second oven. Usually, the pudding I wanted to cook required a different oven temperature from the main course. Recently it occurred to me that the slow cooker cooks some absolutely fabulous puddings to perfection — and this frees up the oven.

The puddings here are ones I serve frequently. Even though most take an hour or two to cook, they can be assembled very quickly and left to cook quietly while you prepare the rest of the meal.

Timing is not crucial — half an hour more usually doesn't matter. Several of the puddings are at their best if allowed to cool a little before serving, allowing the flavours to develop.

Pudding this way is an easy option. Most are whizzed together in a food processor or simply stirred together, tipped into a pudding bowl and placed in the slow cooker for several hours, to cook completely unattended. The velvety smoothness of those with a custard component is much enhanced as a result of cooking in a water bath and, of course, the slow cooker is the perfect bain marie.

I have chosen only puddings which the slow cooker cooks superbly well, and they fall into four categories.

Steamed puddings

The slow cooker is the ideal way to cook steamed puddings — effortlessly, and to perfection. The water in the pot does not need to be topped up as it will not boil dry, and it is almost impossible to overcook the pudding.

Fruit

Both fresh and dried fruits are very well suited to the slow cooker's gentle heat. Fresh fruits remain intact without boiling to a pulp, and dried fruits plump up beautifully as they absorb the cooking liquid and its flavours. Long, slow cooking at low temperatures allows the flavours of the various fruits, spices, liqueurs and other seasonings to mingle and the resulting compote is a rich amalgamation of all these flavours, with the pieces of fruit retaining their shape.

Baked custards

The moderate, moist heat of the slow cooker surrounds the container in which the custard is being cooked, allowing the custard to thicken to a velvety smoothness. Intense heat will cause the custard to separate and weep.

Old-fashioned rice puddings

I love these rich, comforting puddings. During the long slow cooking, the grains of rice swell, absorbing all the flavours, and the pudding thickens and becomes lusciously creamy.

For rice puddings, choose rice with a short or round grain and do not wash — packaged rice has been pre-washed.

Serve hot, warm or chilled, perhaps with fresh or stewed fruit, chopped nuts or a crisp biscuit for texture contrast — biscotti is especially good.

Rhubarb Fool with Star Anise and Honey (see p. 206)

All seasons Christmas pudding

This is a scrumptious steamed pudding. One of the reasons for its superb flavour is the mix of dried fruits: the sharp, strong taste of dried apricots, the voluptuousness of figs and the zing of ginger — all give an intensity of flavour. However, other dried fruits may be substituted as long as the total weight is 650 g.

Don't wait until Christmas to try this pudding. Serve it any time!

160 g Central Otago dried apricots, chopped
130 g dried figs, chopped
130 g crystallised ginger, chopped
130 g raisins
100 g sultanas
100 g soft breadcrumbs
150 g flour
190 g dark cane sugar
1 tsp each mixed spice and ground cinnamon
60 g butter
¼ cup golden syrup
1 tsp baking soda
grated zest of 1½ oranges
¼ cup orange juice
2 Tbsp brandy

1. Preheat the slow cooker for 20 minutes.
2. Place trivet inside slow cooker. (Three $2 coins work well.)
3. Choose an 8-cup capacity pudding basin which will fit inside the slow cooker.
4. Line the base of the pudding basin with non-stick baking paper and grease the sides.
5. In a large bowl, mix together dried fruit, breadcrumbs, flour, sugar, spice and cinnamon. Stir well and set aside.
6. Melt butter and golden syrup together. Stir in baking soda, orange zest, juice, brandy, eggs and grated apple. Combine the two mixtures and mix thoroughly.
7. Pack the mixture into the prepared basin. Lightly brush a sheet of foil with oil and tightly cover the basin with this (greased side inward).

8. Using a foil strap (see p. 11), lift the pudding into the slow cooker, place on trivet and add boiling water to come halfway up the side of the basin.
9. Cover with lid and cook according to the times and settings specified.
10. Lift from slow cooker, allow to cool a little, loosen the edges with a knife and turn out. Can be refrigerated for about 6 weeks.
11. Reheat if necessary, allowing 2–3 hours on high.
12. Place on a serving dish and decorate with holly leaves. I thread red jubes and jelly beans on toothpicks and nestle them amongst the leaves. Serve with cream, Greek yoghurt, custard or ice cream.

2 large eggs (size 7) beaten
1 crisp eating apple (180 g), cored, peeled and grated
holly leaves to decorate

SERVES 8–10

CROCKPOT	**high for 6–7 hours**
SLOW COOKER	**high for 6–7 hours**
SPEEDY SLOW COOKER	**high for 5–6 hours**

Apricot and citrus cheesecakes

The rich creaminess and melt-in-the-mouth texture that we expect from a good cheesecake is here in abundance. Light and tangy, these cheesecakes are sweetly, tartly, overwhelmingly delicious.

I think these cheesecakes are wonderful as they are, but seedless grapes or mandarin segments make a delicious accompaniment. When summer fruits are available, strawberries, raspberries and slices of fresh peach or apricot make the cheesecakes even more irresistible.If baking as a single cheesecake, I like to present it turned out. I line the base of the soufflé dish to make this easy to do.

- non-stick cooking spray
- 500 g cottage cheese (do not use light cottage cheese for this recipe)
- 3 large eggs (size 7)
- 100 g caster sugar
- zest of 1 lemon
- 3 Tbsp lemon juice
- 1½ Tbsp Grand Marnier or other orange liqueur
- ½ tsp almond essence
- 3 Tbsp plain flour

1. Turn the slow cooker on to low and pour in enough hot tap water to reach 1 cm up the sides of the slow cooker.
2. Assemble a 5-cup capacity soufflé dish, or 8 x 150 ml ramekins which will fit into the slow cooker in two layers. The top layer of ramekins should not be positioned directly above the ones beneath, but slightly offset.
3. Coat the soufflé dish or ramekins with non-stick cooking spray and line the base of the soufflé dish with non-stick baking paper.
4. Whizz the cottage cheese in a food processor until very smooth, scraping down the sides occasionally. Add the eggs, sugar, lemon zest, lemon juice, orange liqueur and almond essence and process for 10 seconds or until well combined.

5. Mix the flour through the apricots (this stops them sinking) then fold apricots and flour into the cottage cheese mixture.
6. Divide mixture among prepared ramekins or spoon into the soufflé dish. Do not cover with foil. Place the ramekins inside the slow cooker, positioning them as described above.
7. Cover with lid and cook according to the times and settings specified, or until set. The small individual cheesecakes will cook in approximately 1¾ hours and the large one will take approximately 2½ hours. The centre of the cheesecake should be lightly set and not wobble when the dish is shaken. The cheesecake will continue to cook in its own heat and thicken a little more as it cools. Don't overcook.
8. Remove from the slow cooker and cool. Cover and chill for at least 2 hours before serving. The cheesecakes will keep for up to 3 days in the refrigerator. Serve at room temperature, with fruit if desired.

100 g Central Otago dried apricots, finely diced

SERVES 6–8

CROCKPOT	**low for 1¾–2½ hours**
SLOW COOKER	**low for 1¾–2½ hours**
SPEEDY SLOW COOKER	**low for 1 hour**

Spiced wine fruit salad

A rather special dessert which is simple to prepare. The fruit plumps up beautifully as it absorbs the spiced syrup. Choose crisp eating apples as their slightly tart flavour contrasts well with the sweetness of the dried fruits. Any dried fruit you prefer can replace the fruits listed.

This can be stored for up to a week in the refrigerator. It freezes well too.

1. Turn the slow cooker to low and pour in the red wine, apple juice, sugar and cinnamon stick, and stir well.
2. Add the apple slices, distributing them evenly.
3. Carefully add the apricots, pineapple, ginger and cranberries so that they cover and submerge the apples.
4. Cover with lid and cook according to the times and settings specified, or until the dried fruits are plump and tender.
5. Allow to cool. Remove the cinnamon stick.
6. When required, place the fruit and syrup into an attractive, shallow serving bowl. Halve the grapes, flick out the seeds if necessary and stir into the fruit salad. Leave for 2 or 3 hours before serving.
7. Serve with cream, ice cream or yoghurt.

1½ cups red wine
1¾ cups clear apple juice
½ cup sugar
½ cinnamon stick
2 large eating apples, peeled, cored and thickly sliced
150 g Central Otago dried apricots, sliced
100 g crystallised pineapple, chopped
100 g crystallised ginger, chopped
100g dried cranberries
300 g grapes, seedless

SERVES 8

CROCKPOT	**low for 5–6 hours**
SLOW COOKER	**low for 4½–5½ hours**
SPEEDY SLOW COOKER	**low for 3½ hours**

Chocolate and coconut pudding with a hint of lime

This is a delicious, self-saucing pudding which is very easy to make and always a firm favourite. As it cooks, the pudding separates into two layers: a chocolate sponge cake top and a lime and chocolate sauce beneath.

1. Preheat the slow cooker for 20 minutes.
2. Place trivet inside the slow cooker. (Three $2 coins work well.)
3. Lightly grease a 5-cup capacity casserole dish or a fixed-base cake tin which will fit into the slow cooker. Put the kettle on for boiling water.
4. Make the pudding: sift flour, baking powder and cocoa powder into a medium-sized bowl. Add sugar and coconut and mix well.
5. In another bowl, beat together melted butter, milk and egg and stir this mixture into the dry ingredients. Spoon into the prepared casserole dish.
6. Sift cocoa powder, stir together with brown sugar and sprinkle evenly over the top of the pudding.
7. Pour the boiling water into a heat-proof jug, and add the lime juice. Stir and carefully pour this over the pudding. Cover tightly with foil.
8. Using a foil strap (see p. 11), lift the casserole dish into the slow cooker and place on the trivet.

for the pudding

150 g plain flour

2 tsp baking powder

3 Tbsp cocoa powder

50 g sugar

¼ cup desiccated coconut

40 g butter, melted

⅔ cup standard milk

1 large egg (size 7)

9. Pour enough boiling water into the slow cooker to come halfway up the sides of the casserole dish. Cover with lid and cook according to the times and settings specified. The pudding is cooked when the centre has puffed up and the pudding feels firm to the touch.
10. Using the foil strap, lift the pudding from the slow cooker.
11. Serve hot or warm with yoghurt, cream or ice cream.

CROCKPOT	**high for 2½–3 hours**
SLOW COOKER	**high for 2½–3 hours**
SPEEDY SLOW COOKER	**high for 2¼–3 hours**

for the sauce

2 Tbsp cocoa powder

160 g dark brown sugar

250 ml boiling water

3 Tbsp lime juice

SERVES 6

Cointreau and apricot bread and butter pudding

Forget nursery puddings, this is strictly for grown-ups and has a definite kick. This is gorgeously light, velvety smooth and comforting. The quality of the bread is important. Choose top-of-the-range white bread.

Any orange-based liqueur would be suitable. If making this for the family substitute orange juice for the liqueur.

If more convenient, assemble the pudding earlier in the day and chill in the refrigerator. When ready to cook, return to room temperature before commencing cooking. I think this pudding is at its best when served just warm.

80 g Central Otago dried apricots, sliced thinly
70 g raisins
¼ cup Cointreau or orange juice
220 g crustless bread
1 Tbsp butter, melted
60 g sugar
⅓ cup apricot jam
4 large eggs
2½ cups standard milk

1. Preheat the slow cooker for 20 minutes
2. Place trivet inside slow cooker. (Three $2 coins work well.)
3. Butter the base and sides of a 7–8 cup capacity casserole or soufflé dish which will fit inside the slow cooker.
4. Combine the apricots and raisins in a small bowl. Pour the Cointreau over the dried fruit and leave to macerate for as long as possible.
5. Cut the bread into 2.5 cm squares. Place the bread in the prepared casserole dish.
6. Beat together the butter, sugar, apricot jam and eggs until they are thick and creamy and the sugar has dissolved. Add the milk and stir to mix. Pour

this mixture over the bread, add the macerated dried fruits and stir gently to combine.

7. Lightly brush a sheet of foil with oil or butter and tightly cover the casserole dish with the foil (greased side inward).
8. Using a foil strap (see p. 11), lift the casserole dish into the slow cooker and place on the trivet.
9. Pour enough warm water into the slow cooker to come halfway up the sides of the casserole dish. Cover with lid and cook according to the times and settings specified. The pudding is cooked when a skewer inserted in the centre comes out clean.
10. Remove foil. Combine the muscovado sugar and nutmeg and sprinkle over the pudding.
11. Make the Cointreau sauce: put sugar and cornflour in a small saucepan and mix thoroughly.
12. Stir in orange juice, lemon juice and water.
13. Gently bring to the boil, stirring constantly. Reduce heat and simmer for 2–3 minutes.
14. Remove from the heat, stir in the Cointreau and transfer to a small jug.
15. Serve pudding hot, warm or at room temperature with the Cointreau Sauce and a jug of runny cream or thick Greek yoghurt.

CROCKPOT	high for 3–3½ hours
SLOW COOKER	high for 3–3½ hours
SPEEDY SLOW COOKER	low for 2¾–3 hours, high for 2¾–3 hours

for the topping

2 Tbsp muscovado or other brown sugar

½ tsp freshly grated nutmeg

for the Cointreau sauce

½ cup dark brown sugar

2 tsp cornflour

¼ cup orange juice

1 Tbsp lemon juice

¼ cup water

3 Tbsp Cointreau

SERVES 8–10

Crème brûlée

The velvety smooth texture of baked custards is greatly enhanced by being baked in a water bath, and of course the slow cooker is the perfect bain marie.

Crème brûlée, with its rich and creamy custard beneath a crunchy caramel topping, is the most famous of all custards, and may have originated in France as early as the seventeenth century. However, the English also have very early recipes for a similar custard called Burnt Cream. It is delicious, no matter what the name. Serve with fresh or lightly cooked fruit — Rhubarb and Strawberry Sauce (p. 204) would be perfect.

3 large eggs (size 7)
3 Tbsp caster sugar
1 tsp vanilla essence
375 ml can light and creamy evaporated milk
½ cup standard milk

for the topping

⅔ cup caster sugar

SERVES 6

1. Turn the slow cooker to low and pour in enough hot tap water to come 1cm up the sides of the slow cooker.
2. Choose a 5-cup capacity casserole or soufflé dish which will fit into the slow cooker, or 6 small ramekins (½ cup capacity) which will fit into the slow cooker in two layers. The top layer of ramekins is not positioned directly above the one beneath, but is slightly offset.
3. Beat the eggs with caster sugar and vanilla essence until thick and creamy. Add evaporated milk and standard milk and beat until thoroughly blended.
4. Pour into the soufflé dish or ramekins. Do not cover.
5. Arrange the dish or ramekins in the slow cooker.
6. Cover with lid and cook according to the times and settings specified. Small custards will cook more

quickly than a larger one. The centre of the custard should be lightly set and not wobble when the dish is shaken. The custard will continue to cook in its own heat and thicken a little more as it cools.

7. Remove from the slow cooker and chill.
8. Heat the grill. Sprinkle one or two tablespoons of caster sugar evenly over the top of each pudding.
9. Grill as close as possible to the heat for 2–3 minutes until the sugar melts and caramelises. Do not overcook as the custard will bubble through the sugar.
10. Chill again but for no longer than 2 hours, or the caramel topping will lose its crispness and become soggy.

CROCKPOT	**low for 3½–4½ hours**
SLOW COOKER	**low for 3½–4½ hours**
SPEEDY SLOW COOKER	**low for 2–2¼ hours**

Vanilla baked custard

3 large eggs (size 7)
3 Tbsp caster sugar
1 tsp vanilla essence
375 ml can light and creamy evaporated milk
½ cup standard milk

SERVES 6

1. Turn the slow cooker on to low and pour in enough hot tap water to come 1cm up the sides of the slow cooker.
2. Choose a 5-cup capacity casserole or soufflé dish which will fit into the slow cooker, or 6 small ramekins (½ cup capacity) which will fit into the slow cooker in two layers. The top layer of ramekins is not positioned directly above the one beneath, but is slightly offset.
3. Beat the eggs with caster sugar and vanilla essence until thick and creamy. Add evaporated milk and standard milk and beat until thoroughly blended.
4. Pour into the soufflé dish or ramekins. Do not cover.
5. Arrange the dish or ramekins in the slow cooker.
6. Cover with lid and cook according to the times and settings specified. Small custards will cook more quickly than a larger one. The centre of the custard should be lightly set and not wobble when the dish is shaken. The custard will continue to cook in its own heat and thicken a little more as it cools.
7. Remove from the slow cooker and chill.
8. Serve custard on its own, or with a selection of seasonal fresh fruits.

CROCKPOT	low for 3–4½ hours
SLOW COOKER	low for 3–4½ hours
SPEEDY SLOW COOKER	low for 2–2¼ hours

Coconut custard

This custard is delicately smooth, creamy-rich and magical. Good by itself and superb with fruit, especially tropical fruits.

3 large eggs (size 7)
4 Tbsp (50 g) grated palm sugar or light brown sugar
1 x 400 g can coconut cream (not light)
few drops rose water (optional)
2 Tbsp chopped, unsalted pistachios or lime rind to decorate

SERVES 4–5

1. Turn the slow cooker on to low and pour in enough hot tap water to come 1 cm up the sides of the cooker.
2. Choose a 4-cup capacity casserole or soufflé dish which will fit inside the slow cooker, or 5 ramekins (½ cup capacity) which will fit inside the slow cooker in two layers. The top layer of ramekins is not positioned directly above the layer beneath, but is slightly offset.
3. Beat eggs with palm sugar until thick and creamy. Add coconut cream and beat until thoroughly blended. Stir in the rose water if desired.
4. Pour mixture into the soufflé dish or ramekins. Do not cover. Place dish or dishes in slow cooker.
5. Cover with lid and cook according to the times and settings specified, or until set. Small custards will cook more quickly than a larger one. The centre of the custard should be lightly set and not wobble when the dish is shaken.
6. Remove from the slow cooker and chill. To serve, decorate with pistachios or lime rind.

CROCKPOT	low for 3–4 hours
SLOW COOKER	low for 3–4 hours
SPEEDY SLOW COOKER	low for 2–2¼ hours

Golden syrup pudding

This glorious steamed pudding is feather-light, moist and simple to make. The sharpness of the lemon counteracts the sweetness of the syrup.

1. Preheat the slow cooker on high for 20 minutes.
2. Place trivet inside slow cooker. (Three $2 coins work well.)
3. Lightly grease a 7–8-cup capacity heat-proof basin which will fit inside the slow cooker.
4. Assemble the topping first: put golden syrup into the pudding basin and add lemon juice. Set aside.
5. Make the sponge: place butter, sugar, eggs, golden syrup, flour, yoghurt and milk in the food processor and whizz together, adding a little more milk if necessary to achieve a thick pouring consistency. Pour the sponge mixture on top of the syrup and lemon juice in the pudding basin.
6. Lightly brush a sheet of foil with oil or butter, and tightly cover the pudding basin with the foil (greased side inward).
7. Using a foil strap (see p. 11), lift the pudding basin into the slow cooker and place on trivet.
8. Pour enough boiling water into the slow cooker to come halfway up the sides of the pudding basin. Cover with lid and cook according to the times and settings specified. The pudding is cooked when it springs back when touched in the centre.
9. Using the foil strap, lift the pudding basin from the slow cooker. Allow to rest for 2 minutes.

for the topping

½ cup golden syrup

4 Tbsp lemon juice

for the sponge

60 g very soft butter

100 g sugar

2 large eggs (size 7)

2 Tbsp golden syrup

180 g self-raising flour

⅔ cup Greek yoghurt

2 Tbsp milk (approx.)

SERVES 6–8

10 Choose a large serving plate with an upturned lip to contain the sauce. Invert the serving plate over the top of the basin and, holding the two firmly together, reverse them. The pudding basin will be hot so cover it with a dry tea towel to protect your hands.

11 Serve with cream, ice cream or yoghurt.

CROCKPOT	**high for 3¼–3¾ hours**
SLOW COOKER	**low for 3–3½ hours**
SPEEDY SLOW COOKER	**low for 3–3¼ hours**

Raspberry and chocolate upside down pudding

I love chocolate, I love raspberries, and this is a divine combination — a superbly moist and intensely flavoured pudding-cake.

1. Preheat the slow cooker for 20 minutes.
2. Place trivet inside the slow cooker. (Three $2 coins work well.)
3. Lightly oil the base and sides of a 5-cup capacity soufflé or casserole dish or fixed-base cake tin which will fit inside the slow cooker.
4. Assemble the topping first: melt the butter in the casserole dish. Spread butter evenly over the base and sprinkle with brown sugar.
5. Scatter the fresh or frozen raspberries over the top.
6. Make the cake: place all the remaining ingredients, except milk and decoration, in a food processor, and process for about 10 seconds until the mixture is smooth. Scrape down the sides of the bowl and process again, very briefly. Add milk, a tablespoon at a time, pulsing after each addition until you have a dough with a soft dropping consistency.
7. To make the cake without using a food processor: beat the sugar, oil, yoghurt, eggs and jam together until thick and creamy. Fold in the combined flour and cocoa powder, and add the milk.

for the topping

2 Tbsp butter

3 Tbsp brown sugar

250 g fresh or frozen raspberries (if frozen, use as they are and do not thaw)

for the cake

100 g dark brown sugar

¼ cup canola oil

⅓ cup plain Greek yoghurt

2 large eggs (size 7)

¼ cup blackcurrant or boysenberry jam

160 g self-raising flour

¼ cup cocoa powder

5–6 Tbsp standard milk

8. Pour or spoon evenly over the raspberries in the casserole dish.
9. Lightly brush a sheet of foil with oil, and tightly cover the casserole dish with the foil (greased side inward).
10. Using a foil strap (see p. 11), lift the dish into the slow cooker and place on trivet. Pour enough boiling water into the slow cooker to come halfway up the sides of the dish.
11. Cover with lid and cook according to the times and settings specified. The cake is cooked when it springs back when touched in the centre.
12. Using the foil strap, lift the casserole dish from the slow cooker. Let the cake rest for 4 or 5 minutes before inverting it onto a serving plate. Cool a little and decorate with fresh raspberries or chocolate. Serve warm or at room temperature with yoghurt or cream.

CROCKPOT	**high for 2½–3½ hours**
SLOW COOKER	**high for 2½–3½ hours**
SPEEDY SLOW COOKER	**high for 2¼–3 hours**

fresh raspberries, if available, or a little grated dark chocolate, to decorate

SERVES 8

Lemon delicious

As this pudding bakes, it separates. The delicate, softly set sponge floats to the top and the sweet, tart, lemon-flavoured sauce sinks to the bottom. It deserves to be served often.

- 4 large eggs (size 7), separated
- 200 g sugar
- 30 g melted butter
- 40 g self-raising flour
- grated zest of 2 lemons
- ½ cup lemon juice
- 1½ cups standard milk

SERVES 6

1. Preheat the slow cooker for 20 minutes. Place trivet in the slow cooker. (Three $2 coins work well.)
2. Lightly butter the sides and base of a deep oven-proof dish (7-cup capacity) which will fit inside the slow cooker.
3. Beat egg yolks, sugar and melted butter together until thick and creamy. On a very slow speed add flour, zest and juice and beat briefly until just mixed. Stir in milk.
4. Beat egg whites until they form stiff peaks. With a large metal spoon carefully fold beaten egg whites into lemon mixture.
5. Pour into prepared dish. Cover tightly with foil. Using a foil strap (see p. 11). Place pudding on trivet. Pour hot water into the slow cooker to come halfway up the dish.
6. Cover with lid and cook according to the times and settings specified. The pudding is cooked when it springs back when touched in the centre.
7. Using the foil strap, lift out the pudding. Cool a little before serving, or serve at room temperature.

CROCKPOT	**high for 3–3½ hours**
SLOW COOKER	**high for 2¾–3¼ hours**
SPEEDY SLOW COOKER	**not recommended as too hot on low**

Baked apples

Choose crisp eating apples as they are less likely to collapse. For a strictly grown-up version, add 3 tablespoons of Cointreau or another orange liqueur to the fruit juice.

6 medium apples (180 g each)
6 dates
¾ cup raisins
¾ cup orange or apple juice
¼ cup firmly packed brown sugar
¼ tsp ground nutmeg
¼ tsp ground cinnamon

SERVES 6

1. Core apples and peel the skin from the top third of each apple.
2. Push a date into the cored base of each apple. Add raisins and pack firmly into the cored apples.
3. Arrange the apples in the slow cooker (they may be stacked on top of each other if necessary) and scatter any remaining raisins around the apples.
4. Pour the juice over and around the apples.
5. Combine the brown sugar, nutmeg and cinnamon and sprinkle over the apples.
6. Cover with lid and cook according to the times and settings specified, or until the apples are tender (depending on size and variety of apple).
7. Serve hot or at room temperature with ice cream or thick yoghurt.

CROCKPOT	low for 6–7 hours
SLOW COOKER	low for 5–6 hours
SPEEDY SLOW COOKER	low for 3½–4 hours

Rhubarb and strawberry sauce

This fruity sauce makes a luscious ice cream topping or can be served by itself topped with a dollop of whipped cream. Don't be tempted to leave out the orange zest as it really enhances the flavour of the strawberries.

350–450 g strawberries, fresh or frozen
500 g rhubarb, trimmed
1 cup sugar
grated zest of one orange

SERVES 4–6

1. Hull the strawberries, if fresh, and thaw if frozen.
2. Split any thick rhubarb stalks in half lengthways then cut all stalks into 1 cm lengths. Combine strawberries with the rhubarb in the slow cooker.
3. Add sugar and grated orange zest and stir to combine.
4. Cover with lid and cook according to the times and settings specified.

CROCKPOT	low for 2–3 hours
SLOW COOKER	low for 1¾–2¼ hours
SPEEDY SLOW COOKER	low for 1¾–2 hours

Rhubarb and honey compote

Delicious with cream or yoghurt, or served with one of the Crockpot custards (pp. 194–7).

1. Cut rhubarb into 2 cm lengths.
2. Put orange juice, honey, caster sugar and star anise into the slow cooker and add rhubarb. Stir.
3. Cover with lid and cook according to the times and settings specified.
4. Allow to cool a little. Spoon into an attractive serving bowl, remove star anise and chill.

800 g rhubarb trimmed
2 Tbsp orange juice
¼ cup honey
60 g caster sugar
1 star anise

SERVES 4

CROCKPOT	**low for 2½–3¼ hours**
SLOW COOKER	**low for 2¼–3 hours**
SPEEDY SLOW COOKER	**low for 1¾–2 hours**

Rhubarb fool with star anise and honey

The sweet sharpness of the honeyed rhubarb is enhanced by the slight tartness of the yoghurt. A wonderfully creamy fool which looks lovely served in stemmed wine glasses.

- 2¼ cups plain unsweetened Greek yoghurt
- 1 quantity of Rhubarb and Honey Compote (p. 205)
- 3 Tbsp raw sugar
- orange zest to garnish

1. Gently stir yoghurt through the Rhubarb and Honey Compote. Sprinkle with sugar and gently fold through.
2. Pile into stemmed wine glasses and chill. Garnish with thin twists of orange zest.
3. Serve as is, or with a crisp biscuit or tiny meringue.

SERVES 6

Poached quinces

Quinces take a long time to cook. Leaving them in a low oven for 4–8 hours is the generally accepted way of poaching them. When cooked in the slow cooker, the cooking time for quinces is approximately 3 hours. As the quinces cook, the colour deepens to a gorgeous, reddish-apricot. The juice remains beautifully clear whilst taking on the apricot hues. The fruit will discolour while you are peeling and slicing, but as the colour deepens during cooking, the discolouration is not important.

This recipe was developed by Jacqui George, daughter of my dear friend and fellow food writer, Mary Browne.

1. Preheat the slow cooker for 20 minutes.
2. Add sugar and boiling water and stir until the sugar is dissolved.
3. Add cinnamon stick, cloves, lemon zest and juice.
4. Peel quinces, and cut each into eighths. Using a sharp knife remove the hard core by cutting downwards onto a board. Discard the cores. Place the quince slices in the syrup in the slow cooker.
5. Cover and cook according to the times and settings specified.

1½ cups sugar
3 cups boiling water
½ cinnamon stick
5 whole cloves
zest and juice of 1 lemon
1.75–2.5 kg (about 5 large) quinces

SERVES 4–6

CROCKPOT	**high for approx 3 hours**
SLOW COOKER	**high for 2¾–3 hours**
SPEEDY SLOW COOKER	**high for 2 hours**

Vanilla rice custard

These simple ingredients come together during the long, slow cooking to create a delicious, golden rice custard.

1. Preheat the cooker for 20 minutes.
2. Place trivet inside the slow cooker (three $2 coins work well).
3. Choose a 5-cup capacity casserole or soufflé dish which will fit inside the slow cooker.
4. Place the unwashed rice in the soufflé dish. Add the milk and vanilla essence and stir. Do not cover.
5. Using a foil strap (see page 11), lift the soufflé dish into the slow cooker and place on trivet.
6. Pour hot water into the slow cooker to come halfway up the sides of the soufflé dish. Cover with lid and cook according to the times and settings specified.
7. 20 minutes prior to the completion of the cooking, beat the eggs or yolks with the second measure of milk and stir into the cooked rice. Add sugar and stir.
8. Cover and cook for 20–25 minutes more, stirring occasionally.
9. Use the foil straps and lift the soufflé dish from the cooker. Grate nutmeg over the top and serve.

CROCKPOT	**high for 3 hours**
SLOW COOKER	**high for 2¾ hours**
SPEEDY SLOW COOKER	**high for 2¾ hours**

130 g short grain rice
3 cups standard milk
1 tsp vanilla essence
1 or 2 eggs or 2 egg yolks
¼ cup milk (second measure)
2–3 Tbsp sugar
grated fresh nutmeg

SERVES 4–5

Rice pudding with bay

This combination of flavours is delicious. Bay leaves release their flavour best when torn. The leaves are easy to remove later.

1. Preheat the cooker for 20 minutes.
2. Place trivet inside the cooker (three $2 coins work well).
3. Choose a 5-cup capacity casserole or soufflé dish which will fit inside the slow cooker.
4. Place the unwashed rice in the soufflé dish. Add the milk, vanilla, bay leaves and orange zest and stir. Do not cover.
5. Using a foil strap (see page 11), lift the soufflé dish into the slow cooker and place on trivet.
6. Pour enough hot tap water into the cooker to come halfway up the sides of the soufflé dish. Cover and cook according to the times and settings specified.
7. The rice should be tender and most of the liquid absorbed. You may find that although the rice is tender it may have clumped a little during cooking.
8. Add the sugar and stir. Leave to sit in the cooker for 5 minutes more to allow all the milk to be absorbed and the pudding to thicken evenly.
9. Using foil strap lift soufflé dish out. Sprinkle with extra zest. Serve hot, warm or chilled.

130 g short grain rice
3 cups standard milk
½ tsp vanilla essence
3 bay leaves (fresh if possible) torn
grated zest of one orange
2–3 Tbsp sugar
extra grated zest to garnish

SERVES 4

CROCKPOT	**high for 3 hours**
SLOW COOKER	**high for 2¾ hours**
SPEEDY SLOW COOKER	**high for 2¾ hours**

Creamy coconut rice pudding

The delicate spiciness of cinnamon and saffron adds an exotic fragrance to this rice pudding.

130 g short grain rice
350 ml standard milk
1x400 ml can light coconut cream
or coconut milk
1 cinnamon stick
pinch of saffron threads
3–4 Tbsp sugar

SERVES 4–5

1. Preheat the cooker for 20 minutes.
2. Place trivet inside the cooker (three $2 coins work well).
3. Choose a 5-cup capacity casserole or soufflé dish which will fit inside the cooker.
4. Place the unwashed rice in the soufflé dish. Add the milk, coconut cream or coconut milk, cinnamon stick and saffron and stir. Do not cover.
5. Using a foil strap (see page 11), lift the soufflé dish into the cooker and place on trivet.
6. Pour enough hot tap water into the cooker to come halfway up the sides of the soufflé dish. Cover and cook according to the times and settings specified.
7. The rice should be tender and most of the liquid absorbed. You may find that although the rice is tender it may have clumped a little during cooking
8. Remove the cinnamon stick. Add the sugar and stir. Leave in the slow cooker for 5 minutes to allow all the milk to be absorbed.
9. Use the foil strap and lift the soufflé dish from the slow cooker.
10. Serve hot, warm or chilled with or without fruit.

CROCKPOT	high for 3 hours
SLOW COOKER	high for 2¾ hours
SPEEDY SLOW COOKER	high for 2¾ hours

Jewelled rice pudding

Choose strongly flavoured fruits such as dried apricots, peaches or crystallised ginger for this delicious pudding.

130 g short grain rice
1 tsp vanilla essence
4 cups standard milk
70 g dried fruits,(½ cup) chopped
2–3 Tbsp sugar

SERVES 4–5

1. Preheat the slow cooker for 20 minutes.
2. Place trivet inside the slow cooker (three $2 coins work well).
3. Choose a 5-cup capacity casserole or soufflé dish which will fit inside the slow cooker.
4. Place the unwashed rice in the soufflé dish. Add the vanilla essence and milk and stir. Do not cover.
5. Using a foil strap (see page 11), lift the soufflé dish into the slow cooker and place on trivet.
6. Pour enough hot tap water into the slow cooker to come halfway up the sides of the soufflé dish. Cover with lid and cook according to the times and settings specified.
7. Thirty minutes prior to the completion of the cooking, stir in the dried fruits and sugar.
8. Cover with lid and cook for the final 30 minutes.
9. When the rice is tender, use the foil strap and lift the soufflé dish from the slow cooker.
10. Serve hot, warm or chilled with or without fruit.

CROCKPOT	**high for 3 hours**
SLOW COOKER	**high for 2¾ hours**
SPEEDY SLOW COOKER	**high for 2¾ hours**

Sticky date pudding with toffee sauce

Lusciously light, but rich and moist too, this pudding which has achieved cult status is a firm favourite. I sometimes serve this as a cake, without the Toffee Sauce.

200 g pitted dates, coarsely chopped (dates chop easily with scissors)
300 ml boiling water
1 tsp baking soda
40 g butter, softened
120 g dark brown sugar
2 large eggs (size 7)
1 tsp vanilla
170 g self-raising flour

1. Preheat the slow cooker for 20 minutes.
2. Place trivet inside slow cooker. (Three $2 coins work well.)
3. Choose a fixed base 20 cm cake tin or a 5-cup capacity soufflé dish which will fit inside the slow cooker.
4. Lightly oil the sides of the cake tin or dish and line the base with non-stick baking paper.
5. Place dates in a heat-proof bowl, pour the boiling water over the top, and add the baking soda. Cool a little. Mash well with a potato masher. Set aside.
6. Beat butter, sugar and eggs with an electric mixer until pale and fluffy. Add vanilla, flour and date mixture and stir to combine. This is quite a wet mixture.
7. Pour into prepared cake tin or dish. Lightly brush a sheet of foil with oil or butter and tightly cover the cake tin or dish with the foil (greased side inward).
8. Using a foil strap (see p. 11), lift the cake tin or dish into the slow cooker and place on trivet.
9. Pour enough boiling water into the slow cooker to come halfway up the sides of the cake tin or dish.

CONTINUED OVER

Cover with lid and cook according to the times and settings specified.

10 The pudding is cooked when a skewer inserted in the centre comes out clean.

11 Using the foil strap, lift the pudding from the slow cooker.

12 Let the pudding rest for 2–3 minutes, then invert onto a serving platter. I prefer to serve this pudding just warm or at room temperature. Serve with Toffee Sauce, and yoghurt or whipped cream.

Toffee sauce

1 Place all the ingredients in a small saucepan. Gently heat, stirring until the butter melts and the sugar has dissolved.

2 Boil for 2–3 minutes until the mixture is syrupy.

3 Pour into a jug or bowl to serve. Sauce can be served hot or cold.

for toffee sauce

50 g butter

½ cup cream

150 g dark cane or muscovado sugar

1 tsp vanilla essence

SERVES 6–8

CROCKPOT	**high for 2½–3 hours**
SLOW COOKER	**high for 2½–3 hours**
SPEEDY SLOW COOKER	**high for 2¼–2¾ hours**

Zesty raisin steamed pudding

This lovely, homely pudding, moist and full flavoured, is much loved by all the family. I have used Earl Grey tea to plump up the raisins, as its Bergamot scent complements the fruit. However other teas could be used if preferred.

150 g raisins
30 g butter, chopped
250 ml hot, strong Earl Grey tea
1 tsp baking soda
1 large egg (size 7)
100 g sugar
¼ cup golden syrup (80 g)
zest of 1 orange
210 g plain flour

SERVES 6

1. Preheat the slow cooker for 20 minutes.
2. Place trivet inside slow cooker. (Three $2 coins work well.)
3. Butter the base and sides of a deep, 5-cup capacity fixed base cake tin or casserole dish which will fit inside the slow cooker. If you wish to turn the pudding out of the container for serving, line the base with non-stick baking paper.
4. Place raisins and butter in a small bowl and pour hot tea over the top. Stir in baking soda and set aside.
5. Beat together egg, sugar, golden syrup and orange zest until thick and creamy. Add the raisin mixture and stir.
6. Tip in flour and stir until evenly mixed. This is quite a moist batter.
7. Pour into the prepared cake tin or casserole dish. Lightly brush a sheet of foil with oil or butter and tightly cover the cake tin or casserole dish with the foil (greased side inward).
8. Using a foil strap (see p. 11), lift the cake tin or casserole dish into the slow cooker and place on trivet.

9 Pour enough boiling water into the slow cooker to come halfway up the sides of the casserole dish.

10 Cover with lid and cook according to the times and settings specified. The pudding is cooked when a skewer inserted in the centre comes out clean.

11 Using the foil strap, lift the pudding from the slow cooker.

12 Turn out onto a serving platter and serve with slightly sweetened yoghurt or whipped cream. A pouring custard flavoured with orange liqueur is delicious with this pudding too.

CROCKPOT	**high for 2½–3 hours**
SLOW COOKER	**high for 2½–3 hours**
SPEEDY SLOW COOKER	**high for 2¼–2¾ hours**

Red Chilli Corn Bread (see p. 224)

Breads and cakes

There may be times when you prefer not to turn the oven on, or you do not have access to an oven. If you are on holiday in a caravan without an oven, it is easy to produce simple, delicious breads, cakes and fruit loaves using a slow cooker.

All baking must be done on high heat and the slow cooker must be preheated for 20 minutes. A straight-sided casserole dish is an ideal container, as is a stainless steel pudding basin. You can also use a cake tin as long as it has a fixed base. Check that your chosen dish will fit comfortably inside the slow cooker.

Pumpernickel bread

Pumpernickel bread is the perfect bread to accompany cheese, salami and beer. It is an unleavened, heavy, dark bread which slices beautifully. This recipe is from the *New Zealand Bread Book* by Mary Browne, Helen Leach and Nancy Titchborne. I have changed the method of cooking to suit the slow cooker.

3 cups rye flour
1 cup kibbled rye
1 cup kibbled wheat
½ tsp salt
2 Tbsp treacle
2 Tbsp cooking oil
¼ cup bran
3 cups boiling water
wholemeal flour for shaping (¾–1 cup)

1. Mix all the ingredients (except the flour for shaping) together to form a thick drop batter. Cover the bowl and leave overnight.
2. Next morning preheat the slow cooker for 20 minutes.
3. Place a trivet inside the slow cooker. (Three $2 coins work well.)
4. Choose a 7-cup capacity cake tin or casserole dish which will fit inside the slow cooker. Line the base of the casserole dish or cake tin with non-stick baking paper.
5. Turn the dough out onto a floured board and add sufficient wholemeal flour for handling the dough. Shape into a loaf.
6. Place the loaf into the prepared container and cover with a round of non-stick baking paper. This will prevent the bread from sticking to the foil. Cover the container tightly with foil.
7. Using a foil strap (see p. 11), lift the container into the slow cooker and place on trivet.

8. Cover with the lid and cook according to the times and settings specified. The loaf should feel firm when touched. Remove foil and baking paper for the last 5 minutes of baking.
9. Lift the container from the slow cooker and blot the top of the loaf with a paper towel. The top may look a little damp but it will dry out.
10. Cool before wrapping in greaseproof paper and then in foil. Refrigerate for 1–2 days before slicing thinly. Store unused portions in the refrigerator.

CROCKPOT	**high for 4½–5 hours**
SLOW COOKER	**high for 4½–5 hours**
SPEEDY SLOW COOKER	**high for 3¾–4 hours**

Boston brown bread

This is an adaptation of a traditional American bread. It is rich and dark with a nutty texture, and is excellent with butter for afternoon tea or school lunches. The leftovers make delicious toast.

1 cup wholemeal flour
1 cup rye flour
1 cup fine cornmeal
2 tsp baking soda
½ tsp salt
¼ cup treacle
¼ cup golden syrup
¼ cup brown sugar, firmly packed
2 Tbsp butter
1½ cups milk
1 Tbsp white vinegar
1 cup raisins

1. Preheat the slow cooker for 20 minutes.
2. Place trivet inside slow cooker. (Three $2 coins work well.)
3. Grease an 8-cup capacity stainless steel basin (the batter should not fill more than two-thirds of the basin) which will fit inside the slow cooker.
4. Combine wholemeal flour, rye flour, cornmeal, baking soda and salt in a large bowl.
5. Melt treacle, golden syrup, sugar and butter until just runny. Remove from heat and add milk and vinegar.
6. Make a well in the centre of the dry ingredients and pour in the treacle milk mixture. Add the raisins. Stir until all ingredients are combined.
7. Pour into the greased basin. Lightly brush a sheet of foil with oil and tightly cover the basin with the foil (greased side inward).
8. Using a foil strap (see p. 11), lift the basin into the slow cooker and place on trivet.
9. Pour enough boiling water into the slow cooker to come halfway up the side of the basin.

10 Cover with lid and cook according to the times and settings specified. The bread is done when a skewer inserted in the centre comes out clean.

11 Using the foil strap, lift the basin from the slow cooker and remove foil.

12 Allow to cool for about 10 minutes. Turn bread out onto a wire rack to cool completely before slicing.

CROCKPOT	**high for 4–5 hours**
SLOW COOKER	**high for 4–5 hours**
SPEEDY SLOW COOKER	**high for 3¾–4 hours**

Red chilli corn bread

This American-style corn bread is a perfect accompaniment to soups, stews and salads. Cornmeal (polenta) gives it an interesting rustic texture, and cream-style corn adds extra flavour and moistness.

130 g plain flour
2 tsp baking powder
½ tsp baking soda
170 g medium or coarse cornmeal (not instant)
50 g tasty cheese, grated
2 large eggs (size 7), beaten
1 cup canned cream-style corn
½ cup plain, unsweetened yoghurt
2 Tbsp canola oil
⅓ cup standard milk
1½ Tbsp brown sugar
¾–1 tsp prepared, chopped chilli
¼ cup finely chopped spring onions or chives

1. Preheat slow cooker for 20 minutes.
2. Place trivet in slow cooker. (Three $2 coins work well.)
3. Choose a fixed base 20 cm cake tin or 5-cup capacity soufflé dish which will fit inside the slow cooker.
4. Lightly oil the sides and line the base with non-stick baking paper.
5. In a bowl place flour, baking powder, baking soda, cornmeal and cheese and mix well.
6. In another bowl combine eggs, cream-style corn, yoghurt, oil, milk, brown sugar and chilli, and beat well.
7. Tip the egg mixture into the dry ingredients. Add the spring onions or chives and stir until just moistened. Too much stirring develops the gluten in the flour and makes for tough bread.
8. Pour this mixture into the prepared cake tin or dish. Lightly brush a sheet of foil with oil and cover the cake tin or dish with the foil, greased side inward.
9. Using a foil strap (see p. 11), lift the cake tin or dish into the slow cooker. Pour enough boiling water around it to reach halfway up the sides of the cake tin or dish.

10 Cover with lid and cook according to the times and settings specified. The bread is done when a skewer inserted in the centre comes out clean.

11 Using the foil strap, lift the cake tin or dish from the slow cooker and remove foil. Allow to cool for about 5 minutes. Loosen edges with a knife. Invert onto a cake rack and allow to cool completely.

12 Serve buttered.

CROCKPOT	**high for 2½–2¾ hours**
SLOW COOKER	**high for 2½–2¾ hours**
SPEEDY SLOW COOKER	**high for approx. 2 hours**

Carrot, ginger and lemon cake

A beautifully moist, rich-tasting cake with a tangy lemon icing.

60 g raisins
¼ cup lemon juice
120 g plain flour
1 tsp baking powder
1 tsp baking soda
1 tsp ground cinnamon
100 g wholemeal flour
170 g raw sugar
250 g grated carrot (grated weight)
100 g crystallised ginger, chopped
2 eggs (size 6), beaten
3 Tbsp canola oil

1. Preheat the slow cooker for 20 minutes.
2. Place trivet in slow cooker. (Three $2 coins work well.)
3. Choose a fixed base 20 cm cake tin or a 5–6 cup capacity casserole dish which will fit inside the slow cooker.
4. Lightly oil the sides and line the base with non-stick baking paper.
5. Place raisins and lemon juice in a small bowl. Stir and leave to soak.
6. Sift flour, baking powder, baking soda and cinnamon into a bowl. Add wholemeal flour and stir well.
7. Combine sugar with grated carrot. Stir in ginger, eggs, oil, raisins and lemon juice.
8. Pour the sugar and carrot mixture into the bowl with the sifted dry ingredients. Mix together well.
9. Spoon the mixture into the cake tin or casserole dish and cover tightly with foil.
10. Using a foil strap (see p. 11), place the cake tin or casserole dish on the trivet inside the slow cooker. Pour enough boiling water into the slow cooker to come about halfway way up the sides of the cake tin or casserole dish.

11 Cover with lid and cook according to the times and settings specified. The cake is done when a skewer inserted in the centre comes out clean.

12 Using the foil strap, lift the cake tin or casserole dish out of the slow cooker, remove the foil and allow to cool for about 10 minutes. Slide a knife between the sides of the cake tin or casserole dish and the cake to loosen it, and turn out onto a cake rack. Allow to cool completely.

13 Make the icing: mix the icing sugar with enough of the lemon juice to make an icing of spreadable consistency.

14 Smooth the icing over the cake and sprinkle with chopped crystallised ginger.

CROCKPOT	**high for 3–4 hours**
SLOW COOKER	**high for 3–3½ hours**
SPEEDY SLOW COOKER	**high for 3 hours**

for lemon icing

1¾ cups icing sugar

2 Tbsp lemon juice (approx.)

crystallised ginger, finely chopped to decorate

SERVES 10

Banana fruit loaf

This loaf is moist and delicious, and needs no buttering.

1. Preheat the slow cooker for 20 minutes. Place trivet in slow cooker. (Three $2 coins work well.)
2. Choose a fixed base 20 cm cake tin or 6-cup capacity casserole dish which will fit inside the cooker.
3. Lightly grease the sides and line the base with non-stick baking paper.
4. Combine sugar and dried fruit in a bowl, add hot tea. Stir in butter. Cool a little. Add baking soda, egg and bananas. Mix well.
5. Add sifted dry ingredients. Stir briefly to combine.
6. Spoon into cake tin. Cover tightly with foil.
7. Using a foil strap (see p. 11), place cake tin on a trivet in the slow cooker. Pour boiling water around it to come halfway up the sides of the cake tin.
8. Cover with lid and cook according to the times and settings specified. The loaf is done when a skewer inserted in the centre comes out clean.
9. Lift the cake tin or dish out of the slow cooker. Remove the foil and allow to cool for about 10 minutes. Loosen edges with knife and invert the loaf onto a cake rack. Allow to cool completely.

150 g sugar
130 g dried mixed fruit
250 ml strong Earl Grey tea, hot
1 Tbsp butter
1 tsp baking soda
1 egg (size 6), beaten
2 small ripe bananas, mashed (¾cup)
½ tsp ground nutmeg
½ tsp mixed spice
260 g flour
2 tsp baking powder

CROCKPOT	**high for 3–3½ hours**
SLOW COOKER	**high for 3–3½ hours**
SPEEDY SLOW COOKER	**high for approx. 2¾ hours**

Interesting extras

Lemon Curd (see p. 230)

Lemon curd

Velvety and tart, this curd is a great preserve to have in the refrigerator. Try it on toasted bagels or on top of a pavlova.

60 g butter

350 g sugar

450 ml lemon juice

4 large eggs (size 7), beaten

MAKES APPROX. 4 X 250 ML JARS

1. Preheat the slow cooker for 20 minutes. Place a trivet in the slow cooker. (Three $2 coins work well.)
2. While slow cooker is heating, melt the butter either in a saucepan (not aluminium) or in the microwave.
3. Stir in the sugar and lemon juice and heat just enough for the sugar to dissolve. Leave to cool for about 10 minutes.
4. Sieve the eggs through a plastic or stainless steel sieve into the sugar and lemon juice mixture.
5. Pour into a 5–6-cup capacity casserole dish which will fit inside the slow cooker. (Stainless steel tends to get too hot so I prefer to use Pyrex or oven-proof china.)
6. Cover the dish tightly with foil. Using a foil strap (see p. 11), lift the casserole dish into the slow cooker and place on trivet. Pour in enough hot tap water to reach halfway up the sides of the casserole dish.
7. Cover with lid and cook for 3–4 hours until the liquid thickens. If convenient, stir once or twice during the cooking time.
8. Pour the lemon curd into clean jars, cover and store in the refrigerator. Use within 4 weeks.

CROCKPOT	**low for 3–4 hours**
SLOW COOKER	**low for 3–4 hours**
SPEEDY SLOW COOKER	**low for 2½–3 hours**

Wholegrain oat porridge

The slow cooker cooks porridge to perfection — smooth and deliciously creamy. The porridge thickens with the long, slow cooking, more than it would if cooked conventionally. It's worth making the effort to organise this before you go to bed — a couple of minutes is all it takes.

The proportion of milk to water can be altered to suit your taste — you can use all milk or all water if you prefer, as long as the liquid totals two cups. Use rolled oats instead of wholegrain oats if preferred.

½ cup wholegrain oats
pinch salt
1 cup milk
1 cup water

SERVES 2

1. Place wholegrain oats in a small casserole dish (4–5-cup capacity). Add salt, milk and water.
2. Cover with foil or a plate.
3. Place on a trivet in the slow cooker. (Three $2 coins work well.) Pour enough cold water into the slow cooker to come halfway up the side of the casserole dish.
4. Cook according to the times and settings specified.
5. Serve with your favourite topping — milk, honey or brown sugar.

CROCKPOT	**low for 8–10 hours**
SLOW COOKER	**low for 8–10 hours**
SPEEDY SLOW COOKER	**low for 7½–8½ hours**

Mulled wine

Mulled wine is a heady drink for a chilly winter's night. This is a beautiful, rich magenta colour and wonderfully aromatic.

1. Preheat the slow cooker for 20 minutes.
2. Rinse or scrub the oranges and stud one with whole cloves.
3. Place the studded orange in the slow cooker and add the warmed cranberry juice, red wine, brandy and sugar. Stir.
4. Break the cinnamon stick in half and add to the slow cooker with the cardamom pods.
5. Cover with lid and cook according to the times and settings specified.
6. To serve, remove the clove-studded orange and the pieces of cinnamon stick.
7. Slice the remaining orange, and float the slices on top of the wine.
8. Ladle wine into warm stemmed glasses.

2 medium oranges
6 whole cloves
2 cups cranberry juice, warmed
4 cups red wine
½ cup brandy
½ cup caster sugar
1 cinnamon stick
5 cardamom pods, lightly crushed

MAKES 8–10 GLASSES

CROCKPOT	**high for 1 hour, reduce to low for 3–4 hours**
SLOW COOKER	**high for 1 hour, reduce to low for 3–4 hours**
SPEEDY SLOW COOKER	**high for 1 hour, reduce to low for 2–3 hours**

Hot spiced cider

The flavours of the pineapple and orange are tantalisingly apparent but not dominant in this spicy mulled cider.

1 orange
1 lemon
8 whole cloves
1 cup orange juice, warmed
1 cup pineapple juice, warmed
1 x 1.5 litre bottle apple cider
¼ cup caster sugar
2 cinnamon sticks

MAKES 10–12 GLASSES

1. Preheat the slow cooker for 20 minutes.
2. Rinse or scrub the orange and lemon. Set lemon aside.
3. Cut the orange into quarters and stud each segment with two cloves.
4. Place orange segments, orange juice, pineapple juice, apple cider and sugar in the slow cooker and stir.
5. Break the cinnamon sticks in half and add to the slow cooker.
6. Cover with lid and cook according to the times and settings specified.
7. Remove the clove-studded orange segments and pieces of cinnamon stick.
8. Slice the lemon and float the slices on top of the cider.
9. Ladle cider into warm stemmed glasses.

CROCKPOT	**high for 1 hour, reduce to low for 3–4 hours**
SLOW COOKER	**high for 1 hour, reduce to low for 3–4 hours**
SPEEDY SLOW COOKER	**high for 1 hour, reduce to low for 2–3 hours**

Measurements

New Zealand standard kitchen measurements

1 teaspoon = 5 ml

1 tablespoon = 15 ml

1 cup = 250 ml

4 cups = 1 litre

Abbreviations

tsp = teaspoon

Tbsp = tablespoon

g = gram

cm = centimetre

°C = degrees Celcius

Household metric conversion table

Grams	Ounces
30	1
60	2
90	3
125	4 (¼ lb)
155	5
185	6
220	7
250	8 (½ lb)
375	12 (¾ lb)
500	16 (1 lb)

Weights and measures equivalents

Flour	4 cups = 500 grams
	2 tablespoons = 15 grams
Sugar	2 cups = 500 grams
	1 tablespoon = 15 grams
Butter	2 cups = 500 grams
	1 tablespoon = 15 grams

Length equivalents

Centimetres	Inches
2.5	1
5	2
18	7
20	8
23	9
25	10

Index

Acknowledgements

I would like to thank Barbara Larson, editor for Random House, for her enthusiastic support and personal encouragement. I wish to express my gratitude to Linda Robertson for her beautifully elegant photographs.

A LONGACRE BOOK published by Random House New Zealand, 18 Poland Road, Glenfield, Auckland, New Zealand

For more information about our titles go to www.randomhouse.co.nz

A catalogue record for this book is available from the National Library of New Zealand

Random House New Zealand is part of the Random House Group
New York London Sydney Auckland Delhi Johannesburg

Thanks to Arthur Barnett Ltd, Dunedin, for supplying additional props for photography.

ISBN 978 1 86979 732 4

First published in 1985 by Whitcoulls Publishers, Christchurch, New Zealand.
Published from 1992 by John McIndoe Ltd, Dunedin, New Zealand.
Published from 2005 by McIndoe Publishers, Dunedin, New Zealand.

First edition published 2010. This revised edition published 2011, reprinted 2014.

Cover design: Carla Sy
Text design: Sarah Elworthy

Printed in China by Everbest Printing Co Ltd